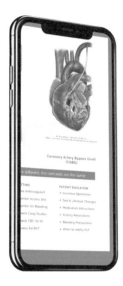
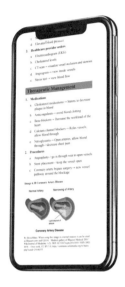

Download Your FREE Digital Copy of this Book at:

NCLEXFlashNotes.com

Disclaimer

Products produced, published or sold by NURSING. com (the term "NURSING.com" refers collectively to TazKai, LLC, NURSING.com, LLC, and NURSING. com Academy, LLC and any other D.B.A. of TazKai, LLC) including but not limited to NURSING.com Academy™, blogs, podcasts, courses, videos, cheatsheets, Scrubcheats™, books, other print and digital materials, and all other products (collectively referred to as the "NURSING.com Products") are for entertainment and informational purposes only and should not be used to make medical diagnosis, give medical advice or prescribe medical treatment.

NURSING.com Products are designed to provide accurate information in regard to the subject matter covered and NURSING.com uses reasonable efforts to ensure such information is accurate. Notwithstanding the foregoing, NURSING.com MAKES NO WARRANTY OR GUARANTEE AS TO, AND ASSUMES NO RESPONSIBILITY FOR, THE CORRECTNESS, SUFFICIENCY, ACCURACY OR COMPLETENESS OF INFORMATION OR RECOMMENDATIONS MADE IN NURSING.COM PRODUCTS, OR FOR ANY ERRORS, OMISSIONS, OR ANY OUTCOMES RELATED TO YOUR USE OF NURSING.COM PRODUCTS.

NURSING.com Products may provide information, guidance, and recommendations related to a variety of subject matters, including but not limited to, medical treatment, emergency care, drugs, medical devices, and side effects; however, research, clinical practice, and government regulations often change the accepted standards and it is SOLELY YOUR RESPONSIBILITY, and not the responsibility of NURSING.com, to determine appropriate medical treatment, the use of any drug in the clinical setting, and for determining FDA status of a drug, reading the package insert, and reviewing prescribing information for the most up-to-date recommendations on dose, precautions, and contraindications, and determining the appropriate usage for a product.

NURSING.com Products were developed based on generally accepted education and nursing principles and standards in the United States, and have not been customized or otherwise specifically designed for use in any other country.

Any procedures and protocols noted in NURSING. com Products are based on current recommendations of responsible sources; however, you understand that other or additional measures may be required under particular circumstances. NURSING.com Products are intended solely as a guide and for educational purposes and are not intended to be used for actual medical treatment or as a statement of the standards of care required in any particular situation, because circumstances and patients' physical conditions can vary widely from one set of circumstances to another.

NURSING.COM PRODUCTS ARE PROVIDED TO YOU "AS IS" AND "AS AVAILABLE", WITHOUT WARRANTY OF ANY KIND, NURSING.COM HEREBY DISCLAIMS ALL WARRANTIES WITH RESPECT TO NURSING.COM PRODUCTS, WHETHER EXPRESS OR IMPLIED, INCLUDING, BUT NOT LIMITED TO, IMPLIED WARRANTIES OF MERCHANTABILITY, FITNESS FOR A PARTICULAR PURPOSE, SATISFACTORY QUALITY OR TITLE, QUIET ENJOYMENT, AND NON-INFRINGEMENT. NO ORAL OR WRITTEN STATEMENT BY ANY EMPLOYEE OR REPRESENTATIVE OF NURSING.COM OR OF ITS SUPPLIERS, LICENSORS AND PARTNERS SHALL CREATE A WARRANTY OR MODIFY THIS SECTION.

YOU EXPRESSLY AGREE THAT YOUR USE OF, OR YOUR INABILITY TO USE, NURSING. COM PRODUCTS IS AT YOUR SOLE RISK. NURSING.COM DOES NOT WARRANT OR ASSUME RESPONSIBILITY FOR THE ACCURACY OR COMPLETENESS OF ANY INFORMATION, TEXT, GRAPHICS, LINKS OR OTHER ITEMS CONTAINED WITHIN NURSING.COM PRODUCTS. NURSING.COM AND ITS SUPPLIERS TAKE PRECAUTIONS TO PROTECT NURSING.COM PRODUCTS, BUT MAKES NO WARRANTIES RESPECTING ANY HARM THAT MAY BE CAUSED BY THE TRANSMISSION OF A COMPUTER VIRUS, WORM, TIME BOMB, LOGIC BOMB, OR OTHER SUCH COMPUTER PROGRAM.

Certain NURSING.com Product's content and material may include facts, views, opinions and recommendations of persons other than NURSING.com, which are deemed by NURSING.com to be of educational interest to NURSING.com Product users. NURSING.com and its suppliers make no guarantee or warranty regarding the accuracy, completeness, or timeliness of such content or material, nor do they make any endorsement in connection with use of such third party content or material. Similarly, statements and opinions in NURSING. com Products are provided as guidelines only and should not be construed as official policy and NURSING.com AND ITS SUPPLIERS EXPRESSLY DISCLAIMS ANY LIABILITY OR RESPONSIBILITY FOR THE CONSEQUENCES OF ANY ACTION TAKEN IN RELIANCE ON THESE STATEMENTS OR OPINIONS.

"you CAN do this"

happy nursing

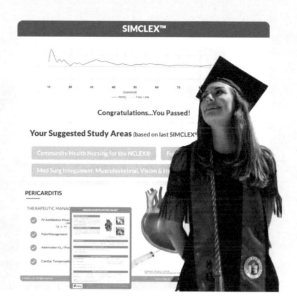

YOU CAN DO THIS!

NURSING.com is clear and concise so you finally learn what you actually need to know!

About the Authors

Jon Haws, BSN, BS, RN, CCRN Alumnus

After graduating nursing school in 2013, Jon Haws began work in a large metropolitan Neuro-ICU, where he served as a bedside nurse, charge nurse, SWAT (rapid response) nurse, and preceptor. He found that through his own experience and working with others that nursing education must change. In 2015, he founded NURSING.com, which transformed into the online nursing education platform known as NURSING.com.

Abby Rose, BSN, RN

Abby has a BS in Nursing from Westminster College. Her nursing education was aided by NURSING.com, and now she is proud to be part of the team! Her nursing career comprises experience from Med-Surg at Salt Lake City's VA Medical Center, Critical Care Nursing in the University of Utah's Cardiovascular ICU, and Huntsman Cancer Hospital's ICU and Chemotherapy Infusion Clinic. In her free time, she spends time with family and friends, explores new recipes, works as a medical aesthetician, stays active and enjoys meeting new dogs.

Kristen Ponichtera, DNP, RN, CCRN

Kristen's nearly 15-year nursing background is multifarious, as it spans from the back of a helicopter to the back of a classroom. Born and raised in intensive care units and emergency departments, Kristen shaped her early experience to become a flight nurse. After serving several years in air medical, she directed her sights towards education, becoming a clinical content/item writer and cditor and academic clinician. She currently serves as nursing faculty at Duke University Health System and Curriculum Manager at NURSING.com

Contributors

Nichole Weaver,
MSN/Ed, RN, CCRN

Sandra Haws, RD

Alitha D. Jones,
MSN/Ed, APRN, AGACNP-BC,
FNP-BC, CCRN-K, CEN, FCCS, LNC
Parkland Hospital

Teri Tench, MSN, RN, CNE
Bon Secours Memorial College of Nursing

Leslie Buck, MSN, RN CPN
Bon Secours Memorial College of Nursing

Debra Ann Culter,
MS, RN, CCRN, CNML, CMSRN
Drexel University

Amy Martinez, MSN, RN, CPN, CNE
Bryant & Stratton College

Meg Highley, MSN, RN, OCN
The James Cancer Hospital and
Solove Research Institute

Ashley Powell, MSN, RN, CPN
Sunderland Royal Hospital, United Kingdom

Maria Stewart, BSN, RN, CCRN, CMSRN
Christus Trinity Mother Frances Louis
Peaches Owen Heart Hospital

Marie Clark, RN, MNHP, C-MSRN

Jason Coco

Fara Ajani, MSN-Ed, RN
Texas Women's University
Parkland Hospital

Jan Ivey MSN, RN, CCRN
Bon Secours Memorial College of Nursing

Crystal Caddell, MSN/Ed, RN
Western Governors University

Lara Ratliff, MSN, RN, WHNP-BC
Bon Secours Memorial College of Nursing

Paige Canaar, MSN, MHA, RN
Genesis Health System

Lindsey Longstreet, BSN, RN
Medical City Healthcare

Kara Tarr, MSN, RN
Duquesne University

Shawntelle Winslow, MSN, BA, RN
State of Delaware Division of Services for Aging
and Adults with Physical Disabilities

Todd Hennig
Content Director, NURSING.com

Table of Contents

Cheatsheet

References

American Academy of Pediatrics (2012). Breastfeeding and the use of human milk. Retrieved from https://pediatrics.aappublications.org/content/129/3/e827.full#content-block

American Heart Association. (2019). Guidelines highlights. Retrieved from https://eccguidelines.heart.org/index.php/guidelines-highlights/

American Psychological Association. (2019). Is willpower a limited resource? Retrieved from https://www.apa.org/helpcenter/willpower-limited-resource.pdf

Baadte, C., & Meinhardt, I. B. (2019). The picture superiority effect in associative memory: A developmental study. *British Journal of Developmental Psychology, 37*(3), 382–395. https://doi-org.wgu.idm.oclc.org/10.1111/bjdp.12280

Google. (2019). Google calendar. Retrieved from https://www.google.com/calendar?

Lee, J. S., Keil, M., & Wong, K. F. E. (2018). Does a tired mind help avoid a decision bias? The effect of ego depletion on escalation of commitment. *Applied Psychology: An International Review, 67*(1), 171–185. https://doi-org.wgu.idm.oclc.org/10.1111/apps.12109

Lucid Chart. (2019). Lucid chart. Retrieved from https://www.lucidchart.com/pages/home

Krathwohl, D. R., & Anderson, L. W. (2010). Merlin C. Wittrock and the Revision of Bloom's Taxonomy. *Educational Psychologist, 45*(1), 64–65. https://doi-org.wgu.idm.oclc.org/10.1080/00461520903433562

Matchu. (2019). Strict workflow google extension. Retrieved from https://chrome.google.com/webstore/detail/strict-workflow/cgmnfnmlficgeijcalkgnnkigkefkbhd?hl=en

National Council of State Boards of Nursing. (2019). Eligibility & licensure/registration requirements. Retrieved from https://www.ncsbn.org/2916.htm

National Council of State Boards of Nursing. (2019). NCLEX-RN® examination test plan for the national council licensure examination for registered nurses. Retrieved from https://www.ncsbn.org/2019_RN_TestPlan-English.pdf

National Council of State Boards of Nursing. (2019). Computerized adaptive testing (CAT). Retrieved from https://www.ncsbn.org/1216.htm

National Council of State Boards of Nursing. (2019). Maximum-length exam rule. Retrieved from https://www.ncsbn.org/5910.htm

National Council of State Boards of Nursing. (2019). Run-out-of-time (R.O.O.T.) rule. Retrieved from https://www.ncsbn.org/5912.htm

Newcombe, N. (2010). Picture this. Retrieved from https://www.aft.org/sites/default/files/periodicals/Newcombe_1.pdf

Newport, Cal. (2016). *Deep Work.* New York, NY:Grand Central Publishing

Nugent, P.M., & Vitale, B. A. (2008). *Test Success: Test-Taking Techniques for Beginning Nursing Students.* Philadelphia, PA: F.A. Davis

Momentumdash.com. (2019). Momentum google extension. Retrieved from https://chrome.google.com/webstore/detail/momentum/laookkfknpbbblfpciffpaejjkokdgca?hl=en

Oregon State University. (2017). Time budget sheet. Retrieved from http://success.oregonstate.edu/sites/success.oregonstate.edu/files/LearningCorner/Tools/time_budget_sheet.pdf

Oregon State University. (2017). Evaluate your study places. Retrieved from http://success.oregonstate.edu/sites/success.oregonstate.edu/files/LearningCorner/Tools/evaluate_your_study_places.pdf

Transfusion Media. (2019). Stayfocusd Google extension. Retrieved from https://chrome.google.com/webstore/detail/stayfocusd/laankejkbhbdhmipfmgcngdelahlfoji?hl=en

Tzu, Sun. (2019). *The Art of War.* Bloomsbury China.

Angina

Overview

Angina is chest pain resulting from inadequate blood flow to the heart muscle. If the flow is not restored, it can lead to further damage.

General

1. **Most common cause**
   a. Coronary artery disease (CAD)
      i. Atherosclerotic plaque ruptures
      ii. Clot forms
2. **Other causes**
   a. Anemia
   b. Heart failure
   c. Stress/overexertion
   d. Abnormal rhythms
3. **Types**
   a. Stable – With exertion. Relieved by nitroglycerin
   b. Unstable – At rest. Lasts longer. Unrelieved by nitroglycerin.
   c. Variant – Unpredictable.
4. **Desired Outcome**
   a. Restore blood flow, decrease chest pain, and improve activity tolerance.

Assessment

1. **Subjective Data**
   a. Chest Pain
   b. Dyspnea on Exertion
2. **Objective Data**
   a. Blood Pressure
      i. Hypotension – ↓ cardiac output
      ii. Hypertension – ↑ stress on the heart
   b. Arrhythmias
      i. Bradycardias - ↓ cardiac output
      ii. Supraventricular Tachycardia - ↑ stress on the heart
      iii. Atrial Fibrillation – ↑ stress on the heart

   c. Other
      i. Syncope
      ii. Pale
      iii. Diaphoretic

Therapeutic Management

1. **Medication Management (anticipated mediations)**
   a. Thienopyridines (clopidogrel)
   b. Heparin
   c. Renin-Angiotensin Blockade (ARBS or Ace inhibitors)
   d. Oxygen
   e. Morphine (only if indicated by facility)
   f. Beta Blockers
   g. Nitroglycerine (per facility policy)
2. **EKG→ Rule out STEMI and monitor arrhythmias**
3. **Monitor Vital Signs (HR, BP, SpO2) for changes**
4. **Cardiac Enzymes→ Determine myocardial damage**
5. **Cardiac Stress Test→ Determine myocardial stress point**
6. **Cluster Care – Rest to decrease myocardial O2 demands**

Image 6.16 Angina Pectoris

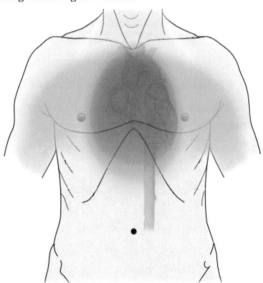

By Ian Furst - Own work derivative of File:Aorta scheme.jpg and File:Gray1220.png, CC BY-SA 3.0, https://commons.wikimedia.org/w/index.php?curid=30655972

Heart Failure

Overview

The heart is a pump, it circulates blood throughout the body. Heart failure = pump failure. Heart failure occurs when the heart cannot pump enough blood to supply the body's needs.

General

1. **Pump Failure→ Decreased perfusion forwards and Increased congestion backward**
2. **Causes**
   a. Myocardial Infarction→ Dead muscle can't pump
   b. Hypertension→ ↑ afterload = ↑ stress on the heart muscle
   c. Valve Disorders=Inefficient pump→ Blood not moving in the right direction
3. **Diagnostics**
   a. BNP (Brain Natriuretic Peptide) → a hormone secreted by cardiomyocytes in response to stretching of the ventricles
   b. Echocardiogram to detect ejection fraction and can diagnose valve disorder
   c. Chest X-Ray to detect cardiomegaly and pulmonary edema
4. **Complications**
   a. Volume Overload
   b. Decreased Perfusion

Assessment

1. **Right-Sided Heart Failure**
   a. Decreased Pulmonary Perfusion
      i. ↓ oxygenation
      ii. ↓ activity tolerance
   b. Increased Systemic Congestion
      i. PERIPHERAL EDEMA
      ii. ↑ Jugular Venous Distention (JVD)
      iii. ↑ Preload
      iv. Weight Gain
      v. Fatigue
      vi. Liver / GI Congestion

2. **Left-Sided Heart Failure**
   a. Decreased Systemic Perfusion
      i. Skin pale or dusky
      ii. ↓ PERIPHERAL PULSES
      iii. Slow capillary refill
      iv. ↓ renal perfusion
         1. ↓ urine output
         2. Kidney Injury / Failure
   b. Increased Pulmonary Congestion
      i. Pulmonary edema
         1. COUGH
         2. PINK/FROTHY SPUTUM
         3. Crackles
         4. Wheezes
         5. Tachypnea
         6. SOB on Exertion
      ii. Anxiety/restlessness

Therapeutic Management

1. **The goal is to decrease the workload on the heart while still increasing cardiac output.**
   a. Decrease Preload
   b. Decrease Afterload
   c. Increase Contractility

Image 6.19 Heart Failure X-Ray

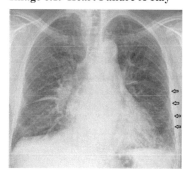

By Mikael Häggström - Own work, CC0, https://commons.wikimedia.org/w/index.php?curid=61595288

R v L HEART FAILURE

Left Ventricle is unable to pump blood into the systemic circulation causing a "back-up" into the pulmonary circulation.

Right Ventricle is unable to pump blood into the pulmonary circulation causing a "back-up" into venous circulation.

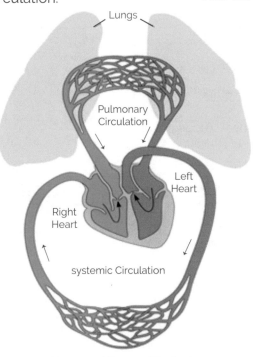

Lungs

Pulmonary Circulation

Left Heart

Right Heart

systemic Circulation

Organs and tissues of the body

Symptoms:

- Shortness of Breath
- Dyspnea on Exertion
- Crackles
- Pink-Frothy Sputum
- Cyanosis
- Fatigue
- Orthopnea
- Tachycardia
- Confusion
- Restlessness

Symptoms:

- Jugular venous Distention
- Fatigue
- Ascites
- Anorexia
- GI distress
- Weight Gain
- Dependent Edema
- Venous Stasis

Coronary Artery Disease

Overview

Coronary artery disease occurs with the buildup of plaque in the main vessels. The primary causes are high blood pressure and cholesterol. The main symptom is chest pain.

General

1. **Major vessels**
   a. Inner walls are damaged
   b. Inflammation occurs→ Plaque sticks to walls and clots form
   c. Blockage → loss of blood supply to the heart
2. **Risk factors**
   a. Smoking
   b. High blood pressure
   c. Obesity
   d. Diabetes
   e. Hyperlipidemia
   f. Family history
3. **Complications**
   a. Acute coronary syndrome→ plaque breaks off and occludes a coronary artery
      i. STEMI (ST-segment elevation myocardial infarction) → "widowmaker"- Near or complete blockage
      ii. NSTEMI (non-ST-Segment elevation myocardial infarction) → Partial blockage
      iii. Unstable angina
      iv. Concerned for → cardiac arrest

Assessment

1. **Presentation**
   a. Chest pain
   b. Arrhythmia
   c. Shortness of breath
   d. Elevated blood pressure

2. **Healthcare provider orders**
   a. Electrocardiogram (EKG)
   b. Cholesterol levels
   c. CT scan→ visualize vessel occlusion and stenosis
   d. Angiogram→ view inside vessels
   e. Stress test→ view blood flow

Therapeutic Management

1. **Medications**
   a. Cholesterol medications→ Statins to decrease plaque in blood
   b. Anticoagulants→ avoid blood clotting
   c. Beta-blockers→ Decrease the workload of the heart
   d. Calcium channel blockers→ Relax vessels, allow blood through
   e. Nitroglycerin→ Open arteries, allow blood through->decrease chest pain
2. **Procedures**
   a. Angioplasty->go in through vein to open vessels
   b. Stent placement->keep the vessel open
   c. Coronary artery bypass surgery→ new vessel pathway around the blockage

Image 6.18 Coronary Artery Disease

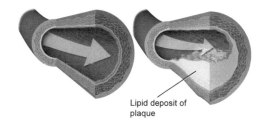

Normal Artery   Narrowing of Artery

Lipid deposit of plaque

Coronary Artery Disease

By BruceBlaus. When using this image in external sources it can be cited as:Blausen.com staff (2014). "Medical gallery of Blausen Medical 2014". WikiJournal of Medicine 1 (2). DOI:10.15347/wjm/2014.010. ISSN 2002-4436. - Own work, CC BY 3.0, https://commons.wikimedia.org/w/index.php?curid=29140355

Hypertension

Assessment

1. **Assessment**
   a. Risk Factors
   b. "Silent Killer" → Asymptomatic until end-organ damage occurs
      1. Stroke
      2. MI
      3. Renal Failure
      4. Heart Failure
   c. Later signs→ Vision changes, frequent headaches, dizziness, and chest pain/angina

Therapeutic Management

1. **Therapeutic Management**
   a. Medication therapy→ ACE Inhibitors, Beta-Blockers, calcium channel blockers, diuretics
   b. Diet & Lifestyle modifications
2. **Nursing Priorities**
   a. Perfusion
      i. Administer BP meds→ CHECK BP/HR FIRST
      ii. Assess for end-organ damage → renal and neuro status
      iii. Strict I&O
      iv. Assess for CV changes

Cardiogenic Shock

Overview

Complete pump failure (heart) causing loss of oxygenated blood flow to the body.

General

1. **Causes**
   a. Myocardial infarction (MI)
   b. End-stage cardiomyopathy
   c. Papillary muscle or valve rupture
   d. Cardiac tamponade
   e. Pulmonary embolism (PE)

Assessment

1. **Sudden, severe, extreme heart failure**
2. **Decreased Perfusion**
   a. ↓ CO, ↓ BP
   b. ↑ HR (compensation)
   c. ↑ SVR (compensation)
   d. Weak, thready pulses (pump isn't pumping effectively and strong)
   e. Cool, diaphoretic skin
   f. Pale, dusky, cyanotic, or mottled skin
   g. ↓ urine output
   h. ↓ LOC, anxiety
3. **Volume Overload (volume backs up because the pump can't pump)**
   a. ↑ CVP
   b. JVD
   c. Pulmonary Edema→ Crackles, pink, frothy sputum, sudden, severe SOB

Therapeutic Management

1. **Treat Cause of the pump failure**
   a. Revascularization for MI (Percutaneous Coronary Intervention, Coronary Artery Bypass Graft)
   b. Thrombolytics or surgical removal for PE
   c. Pericardiocentesis for cardiac tamponade
2. **Improve Contractility**
   a. Dopamine – may ↑ HR
   b. Dobutamine
3. **Decrease Afterload**
   a. Dobutamine
4. **Diuretics**
   a. Furosemide – for Pulmonary edema
   b. Caution – may ↓ BP

Myocardial Infarction

Overview

Sudden restriction of blood supply to a portion of the heart causing ischemia and death to the muscle tissue

General

1. Causes
   a. Coronary Artery Disease and thrombosis

Assessment

1. **Subjective Data**
   a. Chest pain unrelieved by rest
   b. Skin pale, diaphoretic, mottled, nausea, anxiety, SOB, and palpitations that worsen with activity
2. **Objective Data**
   a. Might be hypotensive/bradycardic
   b. ST-elevation on 12-Lead (STEMI)
   c. Elevated Troponins (most sensitive), elevated CK-MB & CK

Therapeutic Management

1. **Medication Management (anticipated mediations)**
   a. Thienopyridines (clopidogrel)
   b. Heparin
   c. Renin-Angiotensin Blockade (ARBS or Ace inhibitors)
   d. Oxygen
   e. Morphine (only if indicated by facility)
   f. Beta Blockers
   g. Nitroglycerine (per facility policy)
2. **Monitor EKG**
3. **Rest – decrease O2 demands of the heart**
4. **Anticipate Provider Orders**

   a. 12-Lead EKG
   b. Cardiac Enzymes q3h x 4
   c. Thrombolytics unless contraindicated
   d. Percutaneous Transluminal Coronary Angioplasty (PTCA)--> opens clogged arteries

Image 6.17 Myocardial Infarction

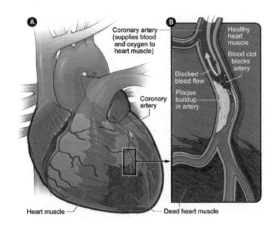

Cheatsheet 6.5 CV Intervention - Nursing Care

CV INTERVENTION - NURSING CARE

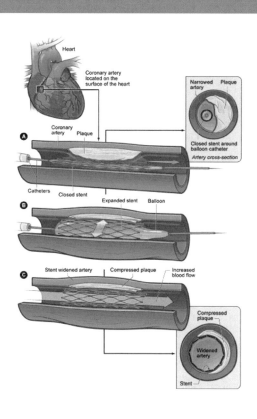

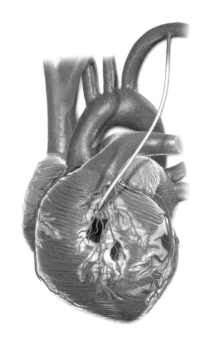

By BruceBlaus - Own work, CC BY 3.0,
https://commons.wikimedia.org/w/index.php?curid=30634272

Percutaneous Coronary Intervention (PCI)

Coronary Artery Bypass Graft (CABG)

Although the procedures are different, the concepts are the same:

PERFUSION
- Pulse Checks
- Vital Signs
- Pain Assessment
- Skin Assessment
- Give BP Meds
- Leg Positioning

CLOTTING
- Give Anticoagulant
- Monitor Access Site
- Monitor for Bleeding
- Check Coag Studies
- Check CBC (H/H)
- Assess for DVT

PATIENT EDUCATION
- Incentive Spirometer
- Diet & Lifestyle Changes
- Medication Instructions
- Activity Restrictions
- Bleeding Precautions
- When to notify HCP

Distributive Shock

Overview

Distributive Shocks – caused by an immune or inflammatory response that interferes with vascular tone, leading to massive peripheral vasodilation.

General

1. **Types**
   a. *Anaphylactic*
      i. Allergic reaction
      ii. Inflammatory cytokines
   b. *Neurogenic*
      i. Spinal cord injury
      ii. Loss of SNS activity
   c. *Septic*
      i. Systemic infection
      ii. Inflammatory cytokines

Assessment

1. **Types**
   a. Anaphylactic
      i. Symptoms
         1. Hives, rash, swelling of arms, trunk, or face/mouth
         2. Exposure to allergen
         3. ↓ SpO2
         4. ↓ BP
         5. ↑ HR
         6. ↑ RR, wheezes
         7. Warm, flushed skin
      ii. Treatment
         1. Epinephrine – relaxes airway muscles
         2. Corticosteroids – ↓ inflammation
         3. Bronchodilators – protect the airway

   b. Neurogenic
      1. Symptoms
         a. Spinal cord injury in the last 24 hours
         b. Warm flushed lower extremities
         c. ↓ BP
         d. ↓ HR (occasional)
         e. Priapism (due to vasodilation)
      2. Treatment
         a. Therapeutic hypothermia = neuroprotective
   c. Septic
      1. Symptoms
         a. ↓ LOC
         b. ↓ BP
         c. ↑ HR
         d. Warm, flushed skin
         e. ↑ Temperature
         f. s/s infection
2. Treatment
   a. IV antibiotics (blood cultures first)
   b. IV fluids to ↑ preload
   c. Corticosteroids only if vasopressors ineffective
   d. Decompensated Shock
      1. Symptoms
         a. Refractory low BP
         b. ↓ LOC
         c. ↓ SpO2
         d. ↓ HR
      2. Treatment
         a. Vasopressors
         b. Intubation for airway protection

Cardiomyopathy

Overview

Abnormality of the heart muscle leads to functional changes

General

1. **Types**
   a. Dilated
      i. 4 chambers enlarged
      ii. Walls thin, less force
      iii. ↓ contractility, ↓ CO
   b. Hypertrophic
      i. Thick ventricle muscle
      ii. Stiff contraction
      iii. Less space to fill
      iv. ↓ Preload, ↓ CO
   c. Restrictive
      i. Ventricles rigid
      ii. Can't stretch to fill
      iii. ↓ SV, ↓ CO

Image 6.21 Cardiomyopathy

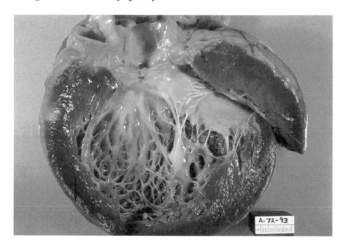

2. **Causes**
   a. Prolonged untreated hypertension
   b. Congestive Heart Failure
   c. Congenital disorders

Assessment

1. **S/S Heart Failure**
   a. Fatigue
   b. SOB
   c. Dysrhythmias
   d. Extra heart sounds (S3/S4)
   e. Poor perfusion
   f. Volume overload (JVD and pulmonary edema)
2. **Echocardiogram or Chest X-ray**
   a. Heart is visibly enlarged or thickened

Therapeutic Management

1. **No cure, only supportive**
2. **Encourage frequent rest**
3. **Minimize Stress**
4. **Manage HTN**
   a. DASH diet
   b. ACE-Inhibitors (Angiotensin-converting enzyme)
   c. ARB's (Angiotensin receptor blockers)
   d. Beta-Blockers
      i. ↓ force of contraction
      ii. ↓ workload
      iii. ↓ O2 demands
5. **Ventricular Assist Devices**
   a. Help eject blood from LV to the aorta

Atrial Fibrillation

Overview

1. **Atrial fibrillation**
   a. Multiple, disorganized cells produce additional electrical impulse in atria
      i. Causes atria to quiver at a fast rate <300 bpm→ The heart is unable to effectively contract which causes pooling of blood in the atria and HIGH risk for stroke
      ii. AV node blocks some of the electrical impulses from reaching the ventricles→ Rapid, irregular ventricular contractions

Image 6.12 Atrial Fibrillation

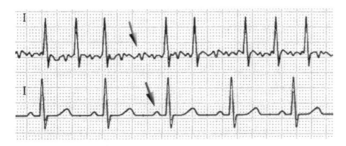

By J. Heuser - Own work, CC BY-SA 3.0, https://commons.wikimedia.org/w/index.php?curid=465397

General

1. **Characteristics of Atrial fibrillation**
   a. Rhythm→ Irregular
   b. Rate→ Atrial rate >300 bpm, Wavy baseline
      i. Ventricular rate→ 60-100 bpm, >100 bpm→ "Rapid Ventricular Rate" (RVR)
   c. P: QRS ratio→ No obvious P waves
   d. A wavy baseline that is not measurable
   e. PR interval→ Not measurable
   f. QRS complex→ 0.06-0.12 seconds

Assessment

1. **Client Presentation**
   a. Palpitations, fatigue, lightheaded/Syncope
2. **Acute or chronic**
   a. If chronic→ Monitor rate/meds
   b. If acute→ Convert to NSR
3. **Atrial and ventricular rates→ RVR**
4. **Decreased Cardiac Output→ Syncope, hypotension**
5. **PT/INR- If taking Coumadin**

Therapeutic Management

1. **Nursing Interventions**
   a. Acute or chronic, 12 Lead EKG, Restore NSR, Assess for s/s of stroke
2. **Control ventricular rate**
   a. Medications
      i. Antiarrhythmics
      ii. Beta-blockers
      iii. Calcium Channel Blockers
   b. Transesophageal echocardiography/ Cardioversion
   c. Ablations
3. **Decrease the risk for stroke**
   a. Anticoagulants→ Coumadin (Warfarin), Xarelto (Rivaroxaban), Eliquis (Apixaban)

Thrombophlebitis

Overview

Thrombus (clot) formation with associated inflammation in extremity.

General

1. **Risk Factors**
   a. *Virchow's Triad*
      i. Venous stasis
      ii. Damage to the inner lining of the vessel
      iii. Hypercoagulability of blood
   b. *Medical History*
      i. History of thrombophlebitis
      ii. Pelvic surgery
      iii. Obesity
      iv. Heart failure, MI
      v. A-fib
      vi. Immobility
      vii. Pregnancy

Assessment

1. **Unilateral findings on the affected side**
   a. Pain
   b. Warm skin
   c. Redness
   d. Tenderness
   e. Febrile state
2. **Confirm clinical picture with diagnostics:**
   a. Ultrasound to visualize
   b. D-Dimer→ product of fibrin degradation present in the blood after a blood clot is degraded by fibrinolysis (positive=clot)

Image 6.22 Thrombophlebitis Symptoms

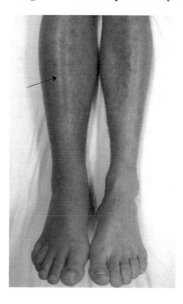

By James Heilman, MD - Own work, CC BY-SA 3.0, https://commons.wikimedia.org/w/index.php?curid=9444797

Therapeutic Management

1. **If the client has confirmed DVT:**
   a. NO SCD/TED, NO massage, Bedrest-->Could dislodge the clot
2. **Initiate anticoagulant therapy**
   a. Heparin→ Monitor PTT q6h
   b. Coumadin (warfarin)--> Monitor PT/INR
3. **IVC filter**
   a. Sits in Inferior Vena Cava
   b. Collects clots before they reach the heart/lungs
   c. Monitor for s/s Emboli
   d. Heart – MI→ Chest Pain
   e. Lungs – Pulmonary Embolism→ Anxiety, SOB, ↑ HR, ↑ RR, chest pain
   f. Brain – Stroke→ Facial droop, arm weakness, speech Difficulty
   g. Monitor distal pulses
   h. Clotting Prevention/Monitoring
      i. Monitor circumference of limb BID
      ii. SCD/TED + enoxaparin sodium (anti-coagulant), if ordered by provider
      iii. Passive ROM
      iv. Early ambulation

Hypovolemic Shock

Overview

1. Hypovolemic Shock – loss of blood volume leading to decreased oxygenation of vital organs
2. The body's compensatory mechanisms fail and organs begin to shut down.

Assessment

1. **Symptoms**
   a. Worsening hypotension→ low volume
   b. Tachycardia→ Body is working hard to pump the volume that is there
   c. Weakness
   d. Tachypnea
   e. Decreased LOC
   f. Inadequate urinary output→ low volume=low output
   g. Weak pulse
   h. The body tries to compensate and if ti can't organ failure occurs
2. **Identify Cause.**
   a. Some causes are vomiting/diarrhea x days, severe burns, traumatic injury, hemorrhage (surgical, obstetric)

Therapeutic Management

1. **Treat Cause**
   a. OR for repair
   b. Meds for vomiting/diarrhea
2. **Replace Volume**
   a. Crystalloid – LR, NS
   b. Colloid – Blood Products
   c. Rapid Infuser
3. **Support Perfusion**
   a. Hemodynamic Monitoring
   b. Vasopressors
4. **Life Support**
   a. Decreased LOC = may need airway protection & ventilation

Sinus Tachycardia

Overview

1. **Characteristics of sinus tachycardia**
   a. Rhythm→ Regular
   b. Heart rate→ >100
   c. P: QRS ratio→ 1:1
   d. PR interval→ 0.12-0.20 seconds
   e. QRS complex→ 0.06-0.12 seconds

Image 6.11 Sinus Tachycardia

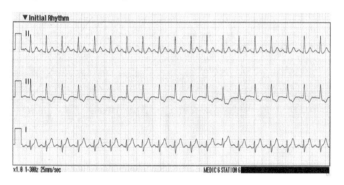

By User:MoodyGroove - en.wikipedia.org, CC BY-SA 3.0, https://commons.wikimedia.org/w/index.php?curid=3961884

General

1. **Client Presentation**
   a. Stable
   b. Unstable→ Rapid heartbeat, palpitations, lightheaded, decreased cardiac output
2. **Cause**
   a. Fever, dehydration, hypotension, anemia, anxiety/fear, pain
3. **Nursing Interventions**
   a. Determine if stable or unstable and treat the cause of tachycardia

Therapeutic Management

1. **Find and treat the cause**
2. **Stable**
   a. Vagal Maneuvers, medications (Beta-Blockers, Calcium Channel Blockers, Adenosine)
3. **Unstable**
   a. Synchronized cardioversion

Cataracts

Overview

A cataract is a clouding of the lens in the eye which leads to a decrease in vision. If left untreated can lead to blindness.

General

1. **Cataract**
   a. The lens has lost transparency and distorts image projected onto the retina
2. **Diagnosis**
   a. Visual acuity testing→ will show a decreased visual acuity
   b. Eye exam→ Will show a cloudy lens

Assessment

1. **Early findings**
   a. Slightly blurred vision, decreased color perception
2. **Later findings**
   a. Blurred vision, double vision, difficulty with ADLs
3. **Vision loss is gradual**
4. **Pupil appears white**

Image 6.88 Congenital Cataracts

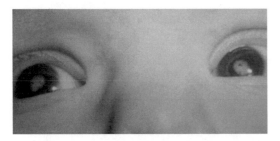

Therapeutic Management

1. **Surgery**
   a. Only curative method
2. **Care post-surgery**
   a. Eye drops several times a day for 2-4 weeks
   b. Mild itching and slight swelling is normal
   c. Pain control
   d. Prevent increases in intraocular pressure
3. **Side effects and complications**
   a. Significant swelling
   b. Bruising
   c. Infection
   d. Pain
   e. Bleeding or increased discharge
   f. Bloodshot sclera
   g. Decreased vision
   h. Flashes of light or floating shapes

Cirrhosis

Overview

1. Chronic, irreversible liver disease
2. Inflammation and fibrosis of liver cells (hepatocytes) leads to the formation of scar tissue within the liver, this causes obstruction of hepatic blood flow and impedes proper liver function

General

1. **Impaired Liver Function**
   a. Liver is sick so it is not functioning properly
      i. Impaired protein metabolism
      ii. Increased drug toxicity because the liver cannot metabolize
      iii. ↓ Coagulation factors, ↑ Ammonia levels, ↑ Bilirubin levels
      iv. ↑ LFT's (ALT, AST, ALP)
      v. Impaired blood sugar regulation
2. **Complications**
   a. Hepatic Encephalopathy→ ↑ Ammonia causes edema in cerebral tissue
   b. Bleeding Risk→ ↓ Clotting factors
   c. Portal Hypertension→ Obstruction of blood flow increases pressure in the portal vein and it backs up into GI circulation
   d. Esophageal Varices→ Dilated, thin veins in the esophagus due to portal hypertension that can rupture and bleed→ Life-threatening emergency

Assessment

1. **Malaise & general fatigue**
2. **Anorexia**
3. **↑ Bilirubin levels**
   a. Jaundice with scleral icterus, dark urine, and clay-colored stools
4. **Impaired protein metabolism**
   a. Causes edema, ascites, and increased ammonia → Hepatic encephalopathy which will present with disorientation, altered LOC, and asterixis (flapping hand tremor)

5. **Inflammation**
   a. Pain in RUQ
   b. Hepatomegaly
   c. Splenomegaly
   d. Portal hypertension
      i. Hemorrhoids
      ii. Varicose Veins
      iii. Esophageal varices that can cause a massive GI bleed and vomiting blood
6. **Impaired Coagulation**
   a. Anemia
   b. Bleeding
   c. Bruising easily

Therapeutic Management

1. **Medications**
   a. Analgesics
   b. Vitamin K for clotting factors
   c. Antacids to ↓ irritation on the esophagus
   d. Lactulose to decrease ammonia levels
   e. Blood products if bleeding
   f. Diuretics to remove fluid
2. **Paracentesis to drain abdominal fluid**
3. **Dietary Restrictions→ Fluid restriction, ↓ Protein intake, ↓ Na intake**
4. **Esophageal Varices**
   a. Endoscopy → cauterize, clip, or band varices to prevent bleeding
   b. Sengstaken-Blakemore OR Minnesota tube – balloon inflated in the esophagus to put pressure on bleeding varices

Cheatsheet 6.14 Cirrhosis Nursing Care

CIRRHOSIS NURSING CARE

CHRONIC, PROGRESSIVE DISEASE OF THE LIVER RESULTING
IN LIVER CELL DESTRUCTION AND SCARRING.

COMPLICATIONS

o **Ascites**
- Fluid accumulation in the peritoneal cavity.
o **Portal Hypertension**
- Elevated pressure in the portal vein because of blood flow obstruction through the liver.
o **Esophageal Variceal Bleeding**
- Blood flow shunts to the weaker veins in the esophagus. These fragile veins can rupture.

o **Hepatic Encephalopathy**
- Accumulation of ammonia due to liver failure can lead to neurologic decline.
o **Hepatorenal Syndrome**
- Renal failure associated with hepatic failure.
o **Coagulation Defects**
- Liver is unable to synthesize coagulation factors making the client prone to bleeding.

MAJOR ASSESSMENT FINDINGS

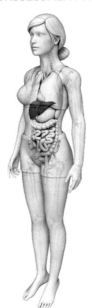

Neurological

Encephalopathy
Asterixis

GI

Ascites
Esophageal Varices
GI Bleeding
Hepatomegaly
Pain
Nausea/Vomiting
Malnutrition

Hematologic

Anemia
DIC
Splenomegaly
Thrombocytopenia

Cardiopulmonary

Fatigue
Spider Angioma
Edema
Portal Hypertension
Dyspnea
Hypoxemia
Hyperventilation

Integumentary

Jaundice
Spider Angiomas
Ecchymosis/Petechia

Fluid and Electrolyte

Ascites
Hypokalemia
Water Retention
Edema

NURSING CARE

Administer	Monitor	Prepare	Other
Supplemental Vitamins	Edema	Patient for Paracentesis	Restrict Na
Enteral Feedings	I&O, Weight	Patient for Shunting	Elevate HOB
Diuretics	Level of Consciousness		Gastric Intubation if Indicated
Blood Products	Bleeding		Avoid Hepatotoxic Medications
Lactulose	Coagulation Times		
	Abdominal Girth		

⚠ Peptic Ulcer Disease

General

1. **Causes**
   a. Helicobacter pylori, frequent use of NSAIDs, smoking, and alcohol use
2. **Diagnosis is done with an upper GI Series x-rays or EGD (Esophagogastroduodenoscopy)**

Image 6.44 Peptic Ulcer Disease

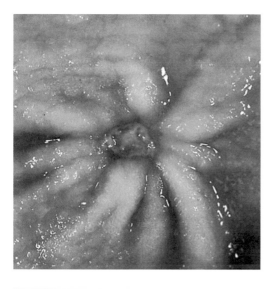

Assessment

1. **Nausea/Vomiting**
2. **Abdominal Pain**
   a. Usually upper abdominal pain
   b. Often burning or sharp pain
   c. Gastric Ulcer→ Gnawing, sharp 30-60 minutes after a meal
   d. Duodenal Ulcer→ 1.5 to 3 hours after eating, pain may also be relieved by eating
3. **Hematemesis (gastric)**
   a. Vomiting of blood
4. **Melena (duodenal)**
   a. Dark black tarry feces

Therapeutic Management

1. Avoid aspirin and NSAIDs because they increase bleeding risk
2. Monitor H&H and assess for bleeding
3. Medications→ H2 receptor antagonists, proton pump inhibitors, antacids, and sucralfate (Carafate) → take 30-60 minutes before meals
4. Surgical options
   a. Vagotomy→ Cut Vagus nerves, ↓ Parasympathetic response= ↓ gastric acid secretion
   b. Gastric resection / Gastrectomy→ Remove all or part of the stomach to remove ulcerated tissue
   c. Billroth I, Billroth II→ Remove a portion of the stomach and reattach to the duodenum (I) or jejunum (II)
   d. Post-Op:
      i. HOB 45°
      ii. Clear Liquids x 3-7 days
      iii. Assess Bowel sounds
      iv. To help the risk for Dumping Syndrome (rapid influx of gastric contents into the small intestine) avoid sugar or fatty foods, eat smaller meals, and do not consume fluids with meals

Cholecystitis

Overview

1. **Acute or chronic inflammation of the gallbladder.**
   a. It is caused by cholelithiasis (gallstones), duct obstruction, and infection
2. **Gallbladder stores and secretes bile into the duodenum to aid in digestion of fats**
3. **Uncorrected can lead to liver damage**
   a. Assessment
   b. N/V
   c. RUQ pain→ Occurs 2-4 hours after high fat meals and lasts 1-3 hours
   d. Murphy's Sign
      i. Pain with expiration while examiners hand is placed below the costal margin on right side at midclavicular line.
      ii. The client then asked to inspire and if the client is unable to inspire due to pain, the test is positive.
   e. Rebound tenderness over RUQ

Image 6.47 Cholecystitis

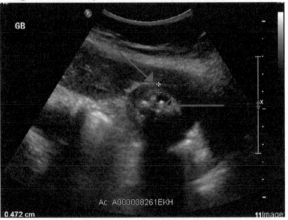

By James Heilman, MD - Own work, CC BY-SA 3.0, https://commons.wikimedia.org/w/index.php?curid=15996764

Therapeutic Management

1. Decrease gallbladder stimulation→ NPO, nasogastric decompression, avoid gas-forming foods
2. Antiemetics, analgesics
3. Cholecystectomy
   a. Removal of gallbladder
   b. Abdominal splinting when coughing
   c. Clear liquids post-op, advance as tolerated/ordered
   d. T-tube drainage
      i. Maintain patency of the duct
      ii. High Fowler's position
      iii. Report drainage >500mL

Inflammatory Bowel Disease

Overview

Autoimmune inflammatory conditions affecting the GI tract, periods of remissions and exacerbations occur

General

1. **Ulcerative Colitis**
   a. Affects colon and rectum
   b. Poor absorption of nutrients
   c. Edema + Lesions + Ulcers
   d. 10-20 Stools/day→ Blood & mucus
   e. Avoid foods that may exacerbate symptoms
      i. Raw vegetables and fruits, nuts, popcorn, whole-grains, cereals, and spicy foods

2. **Crohn's**
   a. Affects entire GI tract
   b. May affect other body systems (especially skin and lymphatic system)
   c. Thickening + scarring + abscesses
   d. 5-6 Stools/day→ Pus & mucus

Image 6.46 Comparison of Inflammatory Bowel Diseases

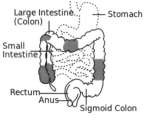
Crohn's Disease

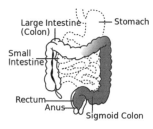
Colitis ulcerosa

By Own work - google search: "crohn Colitis ulcerosa", CC BY-SA 3.0, https://commons.wikimedia.org/w/index.php?curid=39701853

Therapeutic Management

1. **Major medication classes**
   a. Corticosteroids→ ie. Methylprednisolone
      i. Decreases inflammation
      ii. The risk for Cushing's Syndrome with chronic use
   b. Salicylates→ i.e. Sulfasalazine
      i. Inhibits pro-inflammatory chemicals (prostaglandins, interleukin-I, Tumor Necrosis Factor)
   c. Immunomodulators→ i.e. Azathioprine or Methotrexate
      i. Decreases immune and inflammatory response
      ii. Helps decrease the need for corticosteroids
   d. Antidiarrheals→ i.e. Loperamide
      i. Decrease loss of fluid and electrolytes

2. **Surgical options**
   a. Bowel resection or Colectomy
      i. Ulcerative Colitis – curative
      ii. Crohn's – palliative
   b. Surgical removal of abscesses

Cheatsheet 6.12 Colostomy Care

COLOSTOMY CARE

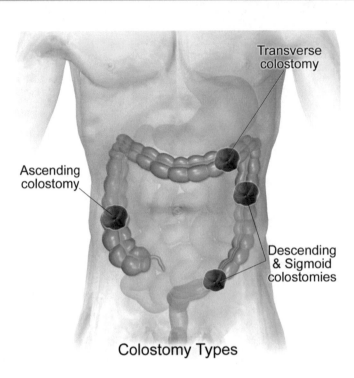

Colostomy Types

Stoma Locations

Patient Care	Patient Care
Assess stoma apperance. Normal color is pink to red. Report stoma that is pale, dark, purple or brown.	Special attention needs to be paid to client diet:
Stoma appliance (bag) should be cut 1/16 - 1/8 in larger than the stoma.	Foods that increase gas: beer, broccoli, brussel sprouts, cabbage, carbonated drinks, beans, dairy, spinach
Cleanse stomal area and keep dry.	Foods that thicken stool: applesauce, banana, bread, cheese, yogurt, rice, pasta
Apply skin barrier before applying appliance.	A small needle sized hole can be made in the pouch to allow flatus to escape. Seal with a bandaid.
Empty appliance frequently to avoid complications. Generally when 1/3 full.	

By BruceBlaus. When using this image in external sources it can be cited as:Blausen.com staff. "Blausen gallery 2014".
Wikiversity Journal of Medicine. DOI:10.15347/wjm/2014.010. ISSN 20018762. - Own work, CC BY 3.0, https://commons.wikimedia.org/w/index.php?curid=33041231

Cheatsheet 6.13 Ulcerative Colitis vs. Crohn's Disease

ULCERATIVE COLITIS VS. CROHN'S DISEASE

Crohn's Disease and Ulcerative Colitis are two forms of Inflammatory Bowel Disease - autoimmune diseases affecting the GI tract. Here's how to tell them apart:

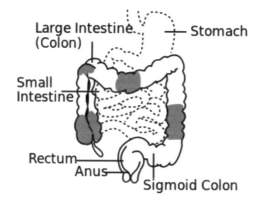

Crohn's Disease

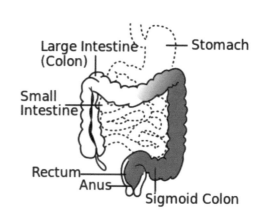

Colitis ulcerosa

By Own work - google search: "crohn Colitis ulcerosa", CC BY-SA 3.0, https://commons.wikimedia.org/w/index.php?curid=39701853

CROHN'S DISEASE:

- Affects entire GI tract
- May affect other body systems
  - Especially skin & lymphatic system
- Thickening + Scarring + Abscesses
- 5-6 Stools/day
  - Pus & mucus

ULCERATIVE COLITIS:

- Affects colon & rectum
  - Progressive from rectum to cecum
- Poor absorption of nutrients
- Edema + Lesions + Ulcers
- 10-20 Stools/day
  - Blood & mucus

Appendicitis

General

1. Unknown exact cause
2. Major risk is rupture → pus and possibly fecal matter spill into peritoneum causing peritonitis, and sepsis

Assessment

1. Abdominal pain at McBurney's point
2. Pain descends to RLQ
3. rebound tenderness
4. ↑ WBC, fever
5. Fever
6. Abdominal guarding
7. SUDDEN RELIEF OF PAIN SIGNIFIES A RUPTURE→ Medical emergency and requires surgical intervention immediately

Image 6.45 McBurney's Point - Appendicitis

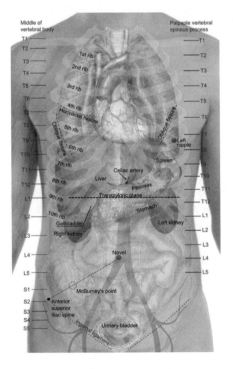

Therapeutic Management

1. Avoid heat application which can lead to rupture
2. Avoid stimulation of peristalsis so keep NPO
3. May require Appendectomy--? Keep NPO
   a. NG tube for decompression
   b. Post-Op Care → Monitor VS, assess for abdominal distention, and clear Liquids, advance diet as tolerated

Pancreatitis

Overview

1. Inflammation of the pancreas
2. Autodigestion of pancreas results from long-term damage

General

1. **Causes**
   a. Alcohol abuse, gallbladder disease, obstruction of the ducts, hyperlipidemia, peptic ulcer disease (PUD)
2. **Types**
   a. Acute – occurs suddenly with most clients recovering fully
   b. Chronic – usually due to long-standing alcohol abuse with loss of pancreatic function

Assessment

1. Abdominal pain with sudden onset, located in the mid epigastric and left upper quadrant
2. N/V
3. Weight loss (malabsorption)
4. Abdominal tenderness
5. Abnormal Labs=↑ WBC, bilirubin, ALP, amylase, lipase
6. Cullen's sign→ Bruising and edema around the umbilicus
7. Turner's sign→ Flank bruising- Indicative of pancreatic autodigestion or retroperitoneal hemorrhage
8. Steatorrhea – fatty, foul-smelling stools

Image 6.43 Cullens Sign in Pancreatitis

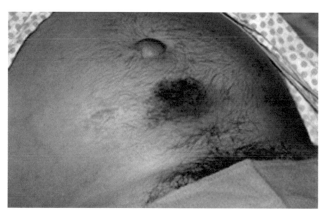

By Herbert L. Fred, MD and Hendrik A. van Dijk - http://cnx.org/content/m14904/latest/, CC BY 2.0, https://commons.wikimedia.org/w/index.php?curid=5038484

Therapeutic Management

1. Suppress Pancreatic secretions through NPO diet and NG tube insertion to decompress the stomach
2. IV hydration
3. TPN for prolonged exacerbations to provide adequate nutrition
4. Endoscopic Retrograde Cholangiopancreatography (ERCP) to remove gallstones→ Camera inserted to visualize common bile duct
5. Surgery
   a. Whipple – remove a portion of pancreas (for mass or tumor)
   b. Pancreatectomy – remove the pancreas, which will require Insulin, glucagon, and pancreatic enzyme supplementation
   c. Cholecystectomy – if the source is gallbladder disease
6. Medications for pain and to control symptoms→ Analgesics, H2 blockers, proton pump inhibitors, insulin, and anticholinergics

Hepatitis

General

1. **Hepatitis A (HAV)**
   a. Health care workers at risk
   b. Transmission is fecal-oral, person-to-person, and poorly washed hands/utensils
   c. Most contagious 10-14 days prior to the onset of symptoms and is self-limiting
   d. Prevention→ strict hand washing, Standard precautions, and Hepatitis A vaccine

2. **Hepatitis B (HBV)**
   a. Transmission by blood or body fluids through IV drug use, sexual contact, or needle Stick
   b. Prevention→ Standard Precautions, hand washing, blood screening, Hepatitis B vaccine, needle precautions, safe sex practices

3. **Hepatitis C (HCV)**
   a. Transmission→ Blood-borne, IV drug users, needle Stick
   b. Prevention→ Standard precautions, needle safety, blood screening, NO Vaccine available

4. **Hepatitis D (HDV)**
   a. Opportunistic infection associated with Hepatitis B Virus (HBV)

5. **Hepatitis E (HEV)**
   a. Fecal/Oral route of transmission, common in underdeveloped countries

Assessment

1. Preicteric Stage→ Flu-like symptoms, pain, and low-grade fever
2. Icteric Stage
   a. ↑ Bilirubin→ causes jaundiced skin & eyes, dark urine, and pruritus
   b. Clay-colored stool (lack of bile secretion)
   c. Elevated liver function tests (LFT's) → AST, ALT, ALP, and Ammonia
3. Posticteric Stage→ Recovery phase, laboratory values return to normal, pain relief, increased energy

Image 6.48 Ascites in Liver Failure

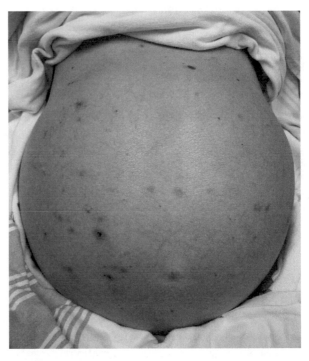

By James Heilman, MD - Own work, CC BY-SA 3.0, https://commons.wikimedia.org/w/index.php?curid=15335623

Image 6.49 Jaundiced Eyes

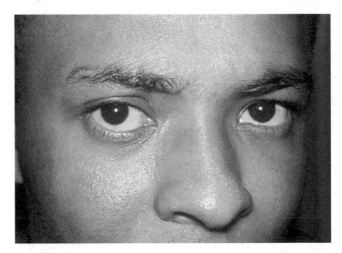

Therapeutic Management

1. **Supportive therapy to address symptoms**
   a. Lactulose for ↑ Ammonia levels
   b. Antiemetics
   c. Antihistamines→ can help treat hep C virus
2. **Antiviral therapy**

Urinary Tract Infection

Overview

1. Infection anywhere within the urinary tract (Kidneys → Ureters → Bladder → Urethra) leading to inflammation
2. Pathogens gain entrance via perineal area or via the bloodstream
    a. Indwelling catheters – Catheter-Associated UTI (CAUTI)
    b. Older males are more prone due to urinary stasis caused by an enlarged prostate

Assessment

1. Urine will be cloudy, strong odor (pyuria), burning with urination, and urinary frequency and will increase
2. Confusion (altered mental status) and lethargy, especially in the elderly
3. ↑ Temp, ↑ WBCs
4. Urine cultures reveal bacteria

Image 6.52 Cloudy Urine in UTI

By James Heilman, MD - Own work, CC BY-SA 3.0, https://commons. wikimedia.org/w/index.php?curid=17978816

Therapeutic Management

1. Urine and Blood cultures BEFORE antimicrobials
2. Antimicrobials
3. Antispasmodic for bladder pain→ Oxybutynin
4. Analgesics→ Pyridium specifically provides relief of pain and burning with urination

Acute Kidney Injury

Overview

1. Sudden onset of renal damage
2. Loss of renal function due to poor circulation or renal cell damage
3. Usually reversible may resolve on its own, but can lead to permanent damage if not reversed quickly

Image 6.50 Kidney Damage

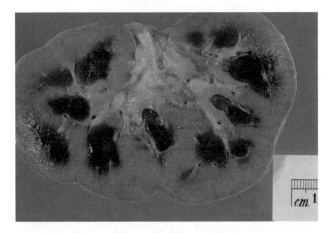

General

1. **Causes**
   a. *Prerenal*
      i. Decreased blood flow to the kidneys, accounts for a majority of cases→ Hypotension, Hypovolemia, ↓ Cardiac Output (i.e. Heart Failure, Shock)
   b. *Intrarenal*
      i. Damage within the kidney itself→ Tubular necrosis, infection, obstruction, contrast dye, nephrotoxic medications
   c. *Postrenal*
      i. Damage between the kidney and urethral meatus backs up, causing damage to kidneys→ due to infection, calculi, or obstruction

2. **Phases**
   a. Onset→ Note a decrease in baseline urine output
   b. Oliguric→ Decreased urine output <400 mL/day. This is the sickest phase where there is a ↑ BUN/Creatinine and ↓ Glomerular Filtration Rate (GFR)
   c. Diuretic→ Beginning to recover, there is a gradual increase in urine output followed by diuresis
   d. Recovery→ has decreased edema, electrolytes normalize, and GFR increases

Assessment

1. Signs and symptoms result from the inability of the kidneys to regulate fluid and electrolytes
2. Azotemia (retention of nitrogen wastes in the blood) → ↑ BUN/Creatinine
3. ↓ Glomerular Filtration Rate (GFR)
4. Decreased urine output in the oliguric phase which should see an increase in diuretic phase
5. Signs of volume overload (HTN, peripheral edema, pulmonary edema)
6. s/s infection if that was the source
7. Metabolic acidosis→ Kidneys not holding HCO3–
8. Electrolyte abnormalities→ ↑ Potassium, ↓ Sodium, ↑ Phosphate, ↓ Calcium

Therapeutic Management

1. **Oliguric Phase**
   a. Restrict fluid intake because there is volume overload, give diuretics for volume overload, and identify & treat the cause
2. **Diuretic Phase**
   a. Replace fluids and electrolytes and especially watch potassium & sodium levels
3. **If not recovering, may need dialysis**

Chronic Kidney Disease

Overview

1. Progressive, irreversible loss of renal function with an associated decline in GFR <60 mL/min
2. All body systems affected
3. Dialysis is required
4. End-Stage Renal Disease (ESRD) = GFR <15 mL/min

General

1. **Causes**
   a. DM, HTN, unreversed acute kidney injury, glomerulonephritis, and autoimmune disorders
2. **Diagnostics**
   a. GFR = Glomerular Filtration Rate
      i. mL / min
      ii. Normal >90 mL/min
   b. Ultrasound shows scarring/damage
   c. ↓ Urine output (could be anuric)
   d. ↑ BUN, Creatinine

Assessment

1. CKD affects every body system
2. Azotemia (buildup of nitrogen in the blood→ urea)--> ↑ BUN, creatinine, uremia
3. Cardiac (related to RAAS effects) → Volume overload, HTN, and CHF
4. Respiratory → Pulmonary edema (vol. overload)
5. Hematologic =↓ erythropoietin so there is anemia and thrombocytopenia
6. Gastrointestinal→ Anorexia (due to Azotemia) and N/V (due to metabolic acidosis)
7. Neurological (cerebral edema & uremic encephalopathy) → Lethargy, confusion, and coma
8. Urinary→ ↓ Urine output and proteinuria (protein leakage because the kidney is not functioning properly)
9. Skeletal→ Osteoporosis occurs because of an imbalance of calcium and phosphorus needed for healthy bones. The kidneys are not functioning and filtering properly.

Therapeutic Management

1. Epoetin alfa = synthetic erythropoietin
2. Avoid administering Aspirin or NSAIDs (risk for interstitial nephritis)
3. Monitor potassium levels
   a. Hyperkalemia → EKG changes (peaked T waves, flat P, wide QRS, blocks, asystole)
   b. Continuous cardiac monitoring
   c. Low potassium diet
   d. Potassium lowering medications (Kayexalate, insulin/dextrose, calcium gluconate)
4. Phosphate binders to lower phosphorus levels→ Given BEFORE meals
5. Calcium supplements to treat the hypocalcemia
6. Hemodialysis or Peritoneal Dialysis

Pelvic Inflammatory Disease

Overview

Pelvic inflammatory disease is an infection of the female reproductive tract, it's caused by alterations in the cervical mucus, which can be fatal if untreated.

General

Overview

1. Infection of reproductive tract → moves to the pelvis and bacteria moves to the uterine cavity and leads to inflammation and scarring
2. Causes→ STDs (most common), vaginal flora overgrowth, infection of pelvic structures
3. Risk factors are risky sexual practice, multiple sexual partners, recent IUD (foreign body) placement, and history of STD
4. Complications→ Infertility, ectopic pregnancy, and sepsis/death

Image 6.55 Pelvic Inflammatory Disease

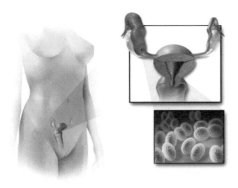

By BruceBlaus. When using this image in external sources it can be cited as:Blausen.com staff (2014). "Medical gallery of Blausen Medical 2014". WikiJournal of Medicine 1 (2). DOI:10.15347/wjm/2014.010. ISSN 2002-4436. - Own work, CC BY 3.0, https://commons.wikimedia.org/w/index.php?curid=30462649

Assessment

1. Assessment
   a. Abdominal pain
   b. Abnormal vaginal bleeding/discharge→ Spotting, yellow or green vaginal discharge
   c. Pain with urination, intercourse
   d. Fever / chills / malaise

Diagnosis

Diagnosis is based on clinical history, physical exam, and lab tests which include gram stain to identify the organism and a culture and sensitivity to choose the right antibiotic

Therapeutic Management

1. Interventions
   a. Antibiotics
   b. Pain control with mild analgesics – NSAIDs
   c. Positioning → Semi-fowler's to help with drainage of infection

Dialysis & Other Renal Points

General

1. **Hemodialysis**
   a. *The purpose is to clear waste and toxins* (urea, creatinine, uric acid) from the blood and regulates electrolytes
   b. *Complications*
      i. Hypotension / Hypovolemic Shock – pulling off 1-4 L of fluid in 2-4 hours
      ii. Air embolus
      iii. Electrolyte Imbalance
      iv. Sepsis
      v. Hemorrhage from site
   c. *Medication Precautions*
      i. HOLD antihypertensives and medications that might drop blood pressure (verify with the provider)
      ii. HOLD medications that will be removed by dialysis (contact pharmacy with questions, verify with the provider)
   d. *Nursing Priorities*
      i. Monitor vital signs and EKG closely throughout (risk for hypotension or EKG changes)
      ii. Monitor labs values closely
      iii. Weigh the client before and after dialysis to estimate fluid loss (1 kg = 1L)
      iv. Assess for bleeding from the site
   e. *Vascular Access*
      i. Types
         1. Graft (artificial 'vessel' loop)
         2. Fistula (allows higher velocity/volume in veins)
         3. External Dialysis Catheter (usually temporary)
      ii. Do NOT insert IVs or take NIBP on the extremity with active fistula or graft
      iii. Assess pulses and capillary refill in the affected extremity
      iv. Monitor fistulas and grafts closely for clots
         1. Bruit: listen for a swooshing sound
         2. Thrill: feel the vibrations
         3. If bruit and thrill are absent notify the provider
      v. Protect Vascular Access → their LIFELINE!

Image 6.53 AV Fistula for Dialysis

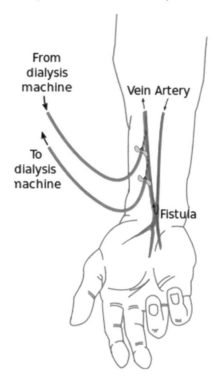

By Kbik at English Wikipedia, CC BY-SA 3.0, https://commons.wikimedia.org/w/index.php?curid=4865832

2. **Peritoneal Dialysis**
   a. Peritoneum acts as a semipermeable membrane for dialysis
      i. Contraindications are peritonitis and abdominal surgery
      ii. Can be continuous (24/7) or intermittent and can be done at home
   b. The client is at risk for peritonitis (infection of the peritoneum) which can be prevented with strict sterile technique and will show as a cloudy outflow

Image 6.54 Peritoneal Dialysis

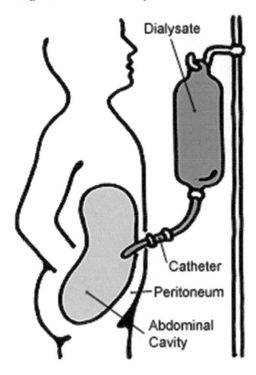

3. **Contrast Dye**
   a. The dye is damaging to kidneys, so fluids should be increased to flush out post-procedure unless contraindicated
   b. Contrast Dye + glucophage (Metformin) = Lactic Acidosis, so hold before CT scan and for 48 hours post-scan

4. **Cystoscopy**
   a. Camera inserted to examine the bladder and take a biopsy
   b. Coagulation studies should be assessed first, then, post-procedure, the site should be assessed for bleeding and pressure applied to the site

Cheatsheet 6.15 Types of Dialysis

TYPES OF DIALYSIS

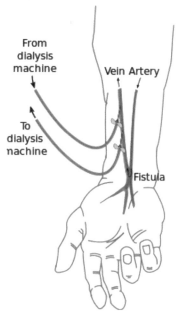

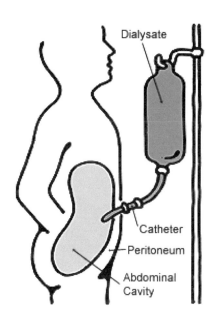

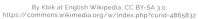
By Kbik at English Wikipedia, CC BY-SA 3.0,
https://commons.wikimedia.org/w/index.php?curid-4865832

Dialysis is the process of using a semipermeable membrane to perform many of the functions of the kidneys that they are no longer able to perform. This includes clearing waste and toxins, removing urea, creatinine, and uric acid, and regulating electrolytes and acid-base balance.

HEMODIALYSIS

Pulls blood from the patient into a machine with a filter, which acts as the semipermeable membrane, then returns the blood to the patient.

- Requires Vascular Access
- Risk for hypovolemic shock

Safety:

- Protect vascular access (Limb Alert - no BP or sticks)
- Pharmacologic considerations
- Monitor VS closely

PERITONEAL DIALYSIS

Instills dialysate fluid into the peritoneum, which acts as the semipermeable membrane, then the fluid is extracted.

- Can be done at home
- Risk for peritonitis

Safety:

- Prevent infection (hand hygiene and sterile technique)
- Monitor for infection (peritonitis)

Menopause

Overview

1. ↓ Reproductive hormones
2. Diagnosed after 12 months of amenorrhea and marks the end of the reproductive period
3. Average around 50 years old

Assessment

1. **Symptoms**
   a. Can start up to 6 years before the final period, and continues for a variable number of years after
   b. Wide range of symptoms
      i. Hot flashes (most common)
      ii. Insomnia
      iii. Weight gain, bloating
      iv. Mood changes, depression
      v. Breast pain, headaches
      vi. Osteoporosis
      vii. Reproductive, urinary changes
         1. Irregular menses
         2. Vaginal dryness, painful intercourse
         3. Prolapse of reproductive and urinary structures

2. **Lab testing seen with endocrine changes**
   i. ↑ FSH→ Indicates that menopause has occurred
   ii. ↓ Estrogen and inhibin

Image 6.56 Menopause

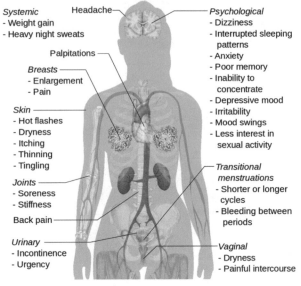

By Mikael Häggström - Own work, CC0, https://commons.wikimedia.org/w/index.php?curid=40969037

Therapeutic Management

1. Hormone replacement therapy for severe cases
2. Symptom management

Blood Transfusions

Overview

1. Four types of products→ Packed Red Blood Cells (PRBCs), cryoprecipitate, fresh frozen plasma, and platelets
2. Must match donor type→ ABO type, Rh status, and special antibodies

General

1. **PRBCs aka "Unit of Blood" → Given for anemia**
2. **FFP (Fresh Frozen Plasma)**
   a. Contains clotting factors
3. **Platelets**
   a. Given for thrombocytopenia and often pre-procedure for clients with Platelets <50. Re-check 1-hour post-transfusion.
4. **Cryoprecipitate**
   a. Contains fibrinogen and is commonly used for hemorrhage and disseminated Intravascular Coagulation (DIC)
5. **Prepare to transfuse**
   a. Type and crossmatch/screen
   b. Pre-transfusion vitals
   c. Administration materials
      i. The special blood IV tubing
      ii. 0.9% normal saline
      iii. Access to emergency medications
6. **Begin transfusion**
   a. Independent double-check completed by two RNs
   b. Initiate infusion at a slow rate for the first 10-15 minutes
   c. Monitor for Reaction
7. **Transfusion Reactions**
   a. Present similarly to anaphylaxis and can occur up to 24 hours after transfusion
8. **Delayed Transfusion Reactions**
   a. Caused by antibody mismatch and can be potentially fatal

Assessment

1. Transfusion reactions most commonly occur in the first 10-15 minutes, and symptoms are pruritus, rash, fever, chills, low back pain, and anxiety
2. Delayed transfusion reactions occur in clients who have received transfusions before, or if there are undetectable antibodies below the threshold of screening
3. Post-Transfusion→ Redraw Complete Blood Count (CBC)

Therapeutic Management

1. **Transfusion Reactions**
   a. Immediately STOP transfusion, SAVE the blood product for lab
   b. Treatment similar to anaphylaxis
      i. Notify provider
      ii. Anti-histamines (diphenhydramine)
      iii. Acetaminophen
      iv. Consider furosemide for fluid overload and to maintain kidney function
   c. Monitor airway patency
   d. Maintain IV access
   e. Report to the blood bank

Acquired Immune Deficiency Syndrome

General

1. A condition caused by the HIV virus (late-stage HIV infection)
2. Interferes with and destroys T4 Lymphocytes, which causes an increase in susceptibility to infection
3. At risk for opportunistic infections/conditions such as tuberculosis, pneumonia, cancers, and candidiasis

Assessment

1. Frequent infections, wasting syndrome, skin breakdown, stomatitis, malnutrition, and dehydration
2. Leukopenia (↓WBCs)
3. Kaposi's sarcoma→ A tumor causes lesions to grow in the skin and lymph nodes, characterized by purple/red lesions on skin and organs
4. Candidiasis in the mouth (thrush)

Therapeutic Management

1. Respiratory support
2. Nutritional support→ Small frequent meals, premedicate to avoid nausea, and provide favorite foods
3. Monitor fluid and electrolyte balance
4. Assess for infection
5. Initiate strict infection control precautions and observe hand hygiene

Image 6.62 Symptoms of AIDS

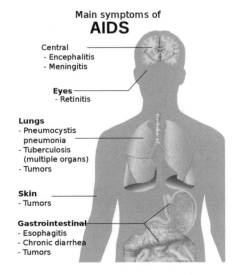

Image 6.63 Symptoms of HIV

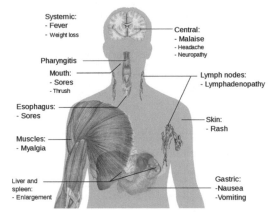

Sickle Cell Anemia

Overview

1. A hereditary disorder that primarily affects African Americans by a recessive trait
   a. If both parents are carriers there is a 25% of their offspring having SCA, 50% chance of being a carrier, and only a 25% chance of no inheritance

General

1. **The genetic mutation leads to rigid, misshapen RBCs**
   a. Affects hemoglobin's ability to carry oxygen and the misshapen RBCs get stuck within the blood vessels, causing an obstruction
2. **Can lead to Sickle Cell Crisis – 2 kinds**
   a. *Micro-occlusions → Vasoocclusive Crisis*
      i. ↓ Blood flow to tissue = hypoxia, ischemia, infarction
         1. Joint pain
         2. Stroke
         3. Acute Chest Syndrome
      ii. Sequestration
         1. Pooling of blood
         2. Usually in spleen
   b. *Acute Exacerbation*
      i. Caused by hypoxia, exercise, high altitude, fever, temperature extreme

Assessment

1. **Pallor and fatigue**
2. **Severe Pain**
   a. Due to micro-occlusions→ Symptoms match the location of the occlusion

Therapeutic Management

1. **Hemodilution**
   a. Dilute blood to 'wash out' sickled cells
   b. Give IV Fluids for hydration
   c. Blood transfusions → give properly shaped/ functioning RBCs
2. **Oxygen Supplementation**
   a. Increase oxygen delivery to the tissues if the client is hypoxic!
3. **Pain Relief→ This pain is severe**
4. **Hydroxyurea**
   a. A medication used for clients with a history of frequent crisis
   b. Shown in infants to increase potential for preserving fetal hemoglobin (a form of Hgb plentiful in gestation), which increases availibility of oxygen to the tissues, thereby reducing complications of SCD

Image 5.3 Sickle Cell Anemia

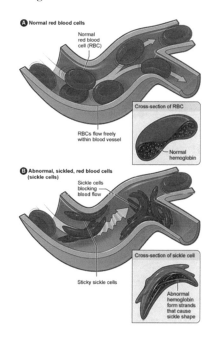

Disseminated Intravascular Coagulation

Overview

Widespread activation of the clotting cascade where the body clots and bleeds, the normal clotting cascade is disrupted and the clotting factors are used up. This causes severe bleeding and massive hemorrhage.

General

Risk Factors – anything that initiates the clotting cascade which then will overreact. The leading cause of DIC is infection.

Assessment

1. Pallor, dyspnea, chest pain, anxiety, confusion
2. Ecchymosis→ Petechiae, purpura, and hematomas
3. Bleeding from every orifice
4. Abnormal Labs show a prolonged PTT, PT, thrombin time, and↓ Platelets
5. Tachycardia and hypotension

Therapeutic Management

1. Determine and treat underlying cause immediately
2. Replace clotting factors, fresh frozen plasma, vitamin K, factor VII
3. Administer Heparin drip if excessive clotting→ This will STOP the consumption of clotting factors

Anaphylaxis

General

Massive allergic response → histamine release from damaged cells causes swelling, inflammation, and massive vasodilation that can lead to distributive shock

Assessment

1. Urticaria (hives)
2. Angioedema (facial swelling) → lips, tongue, mouth, throat, and risk for airway compromise
3. Skin flushing
4. Anaphylactic Shock→ Hypotension and cardiac arrest

Image 6.64 Symptoms of Anaphylaxis

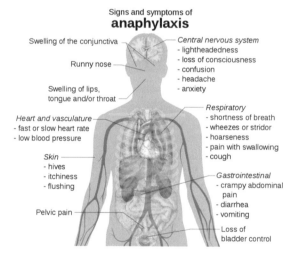

By Mikael Häggström - Own work, CC0, https://commons.wikimedia.org/w/index.php?curid=17700404

Therapeutic Management

1. Monitor respiratory and cardiovascular status
2. Administer Epinephrine IM immediately
   a. Adults – 0.3 mg 1:1000
   b. Children – 0.15 mg 1:1000
   c. EpiPen Auto-injector
   d. Goal = prevent life-threatening airway collapse or shock
3. Administer Oxygen, antihistamines, corticosteroids, and IV fluids as needed to support hemodynamics

Leukemia

Overview

1. The proliferation of abnormal, undeveloped WBCs, which are needed for infection control/immunity
2. Diagnosed by blood tests and bone marrow biopsy

General

1. Characterized by type of WBC affected
   a. Acute Lymphocytic Leukemia (ALL) → 2-4 years of age
   b. Chronic Lymphocytic Leukemia (CLL) → 50-70 years of age
   c. Acute Myelogenous Leukemia (AML) → peaks at 60 years of age
   d. Chronic Myelogenous Leukemia (CML) → Incidence increases with age

Assessment

1. Weight loss
2. Fever
3. Infections
4. Pain in bones and joints
5. Night sweats
6. Aplastic Anemia→ Pallor, fatigue, and easy bleeding and bruising
7. ↑ WBC in CLL and CML
8. ↓ WBC in ALL and AML
9. Philadelphia chromosome in the majority of CML clients
10. Mouth sores from chemo

Therapeutic Management

1. Chemotherapy and radiation
2. Bone Marrow Biopsy→ Apply pressure to the biopsy site
3. Initiate neutropenic precautions (Strict handwashing, limit visitation, no fresh fruits or flowers)
4. Plan activities to provide time for rest
5. Instruct a client on oral hygiene (Rinse mouth with saline, avoid lemon or alcohol-based mouthwashes)

Image 6.58 Leukemia

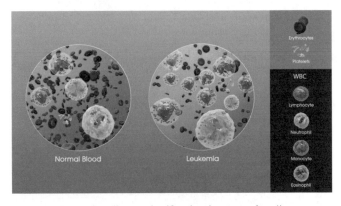

By Manu Sharma, http://www.scientificanimations.com - http://www.scientificanimations.com/wiki-images/, CC BY-SA 4.0, https://commons.wikimedia.org/w/index.php?curid=60957602

Thrombocytopenia

Overview

1. A decrease in the circulating platelets (<100,000/mL)

General

1. **Causes**

   a. Aplastic Anemia which will cause a decreased production

   b. Autoimmune Disorders which will cause an increase in destruction

   c. Medication-induced ie. Heparin-Induced, cytotoxic drugs, some antibiotics

Assessment

1. **Abnormal Labs**

   a. ↓ Platelet count

   b. ↓ Hgb, Hct

2. **Bleeding because there are not enough platelets to clot.**

   a. This will show as petechiae, epistaxis, GI bleeding (Hematemesis, Melena, Occult blood in the stool), hematuria, and hemoptysis

Therapeutic Management

1. Platelet transfusions

2. Bleeding precautions→ Avoid invasive procedure, soft-bristled toothbrush, and avoid medications that interfere with coagulation (i.e. Aspirin, Heparin)

Image 6.57 Petechiae

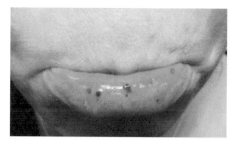

By Mdscottis - Own work, CC BY-SA 3.0, https://commons.wikimedia.org/w/index.php?curid=24734024

Cheatsheet 6.16 Blood Compatibility Chart

BLOOD COMPATIBILITY CHART

	DONOR BLOOD TYPE							
PATIENT BLOOD TYPE	**O-**	**O+**	**B-**	**B+**	**A-**	**A+**	**AB-**	**AB+**
AB+	✓	✓	✓	✓	✓	✓	✓	✓
AB-	✓		✓		✓		✓	
A+	✓	✓			✓	✓		
A-	✓				✓			
B+	✓	✓	✓	✓				
B-	✓		✓					
O+	✓	✓						
O-	✓							

Lymphoma

General

1. Cancer of the lymphatic system affecting lymphocytes, which impairs immune response
2. Classified by Type
   a. Hodgkin's Lymphoma→ Presence of Reed-Sternberg cells
   b. Non-Hodgkin's Lymphoma→ Absence of Reed-Sternberg cells, 90% of Lymphomas
3. Tumors may form in/around the lymph nodes
4. Lymphocytes affected → can travel/metastasize through the lymphatic system

Assessment

1. Painless swelling of lymph nodes
2. Persistent fatigue
3. Fever
4. Night sweats
5. Shortness of breath
6. Unexplained weight loss
7. Enlarged liver or spleen
8. Risk for Infection

Therapeutic Management

1. Official diagnosis with lymph node biopsy→ Hold pressure over the biopsy site
2. Chemotherapy and radiation
3. Monitor for s/s metastasis (high-risk because it travels through the lymphatic system in the body)

Image 6.59 Lymphoma

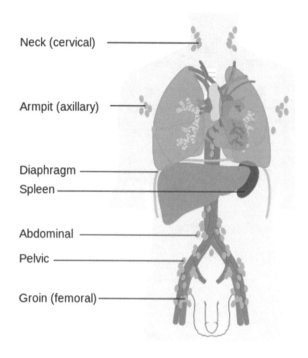

Neck (cervical)
Armpit (axillary)
Diaphragm
Spleen
Abdominal
Pelvic
Groin (femoral)

By Cancer Research UK - Original email from CRUK, CC BY-SA 4.0, https://commons.wikimedia.org/w/index.php?curid=34334121

Cheatsheet 6.17 Cancer Quick Tips

CANCER QUICK TIPS

WARNING SIGNS OF CANCER (CAUTION)

- Change in bowel pattern
- A sore that does not heal
- Unusual bleeding
- Thickening of breast, testicle, skin
- Indigestion
- Obvious change in mole
- Nagging cough

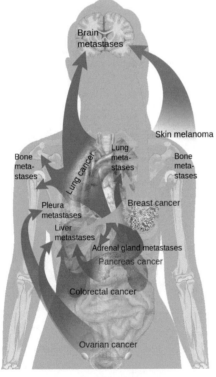

COMMON SITES FOR METASTASIS

CANCER STAGING	
Stage 0	Carcinoma in situ
Stage I	Local tumor growth
Stage II	Limited spreading
Stage III	Regional spreading
Stage IV	Metastasis to other organs

Burn Injuries

General

1. **Degrees**
   a. *First Degree* – skin intact, reddened, painful
   b. *Second Degree* – Partial Thickness, broken skin, pain, pink/red, blisters
   c. *Third Degree* – Full Thickness, often painless, white/black eschar
   d. *Fourth Degree* – Muscle and/or bone exposed. Common in electrical burns.

Image 6.70 Stages of Burns

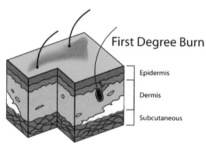

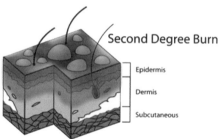

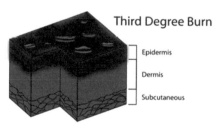

By The original uploader was K. Aainsqatsi at English Wikipedia(Original text: K. Aainsqatsi) - Transferred from en.wikipedia to Commons.(Original text: self-made), CC BY-SA 3.0, https://commons.wikimedia.org/w/index.php?curid=2584650

Image 6.71 First Degree Burn

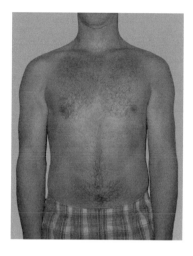

Image 6.72 Second Degree Burn

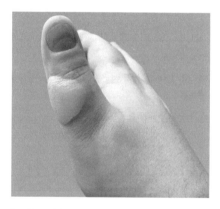

By The original uploader was Snickerdo at English Wikipedia - Transferred from en.wikipedia to Commons., CC BY-SA 3.0, https://commons.wikimedia.org/w/index.php?curid=3358773

Image 6.73 Third Degree Burn

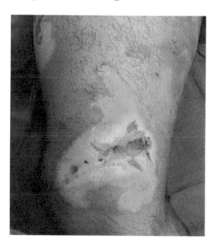

By Clifford Sheckter, Arhana Chattopadhyay, John Paro and Yvonne Karanas - Direct source. Full paper., CC BY 4.0, https://commons.wikimedia.org/w/index.php?curid=68491398

Image 6.74 Fourth Degree Burn

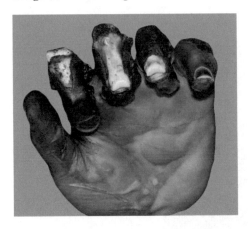

By goga312. Original uploader was Goga312 at ru.wikipedia - Transferred from ru.wikipedia(Original text : собственная работа), CC BY-SA 3.0, https://commons.wikimedia.org/w/index.php?curid=7771672

Assessment

1. On Arrival to ED/Hospital
   a. Determine the total body Surface Area (TBSA) Burned
2. 1st and 2nd degree = very painful
3. 3rd and 4th may be painless due to nerve damage
4. Impaired temperature regulation
5. Hypovolemia due to third spacing/capillary leak so the client will have ↑ HR, ↓BP

Therapeutic Management

1. **Fluid Resuscitation**
   a. Parkland Burn Formula
      i. 4 x TBSA (%) x kg
      ii. Half over 8 hours
      iii. Half over 16 hours
   b. Titrate to Urine Output 30-50 mL/hr
   c. Assess for edema
2. **Administer Antibiotics**
3. **Aggressive Wound Care**
4. **Pain Management – typically with opioid analgesics, PCA if able**
5. **Optimize Nutrition Intake to promote healing**
   a. May require NG Tube for feeds or PICC line for TPN
6. **Skin Grafting**
   a. Autologous – taken from healthy tissue on the client
   b. Allogeneic – another human donor
   c. Meshed and stretched over wound

Cheatsheet 6.21 Burn Staging

BURN STAGING

First Degree

Reddened, painful, intact skin

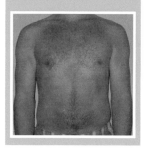

Second Degree

Partial Thickness, broken skin, pain, pink/red, blisters

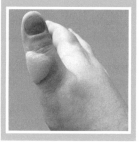

By The original uploader was Snickerdo at English Wikipedia - Transferred from en.wikipedia to Commons.. CC BY-SA 3.0, https://commons.wikimedia.org/w/index.php?curid=3358773

Third Degree

Full thickness, often painless, white/black eschar

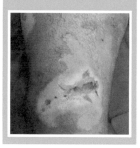

By Clifford Sheckter, Arhana Chattopadhyay, John Paro and Yvonne Karanas - Direct source. Full paper., CC BY 4.0, https://commons.wikimedia.org/w/index.php?curid=68491398

Fourth Degree

Muscle and/or bone exposed. Common in electrical burns

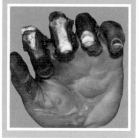

By goga312. Original uploader was Goga312 at ru.wikipedia - Transferred from ru.wikipedia(Original text : собственная работа), CC BY-SA 3.0, https://commons.wikimedia.org/w/index.php?curid=7771672

Herpes Zoster - Shingles

Overview

Viral Infection caused by Herpes Zoster virus

General

1. Most common in elderly clients with a history of chickenpox or the chickenpox vaccine
2. Highly contagious

Assessment

1. Vesicular rash that follows the dermatome and is usually unilateral
2. Painful, itchy
3. Fever, Malaise, Fatigue

Image 6.77 Shingles Progression

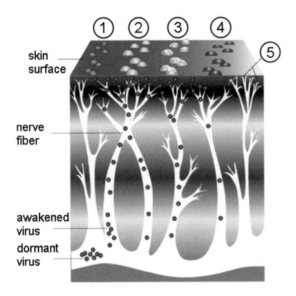

Image 6.78 Shingles Dermatome on Chest

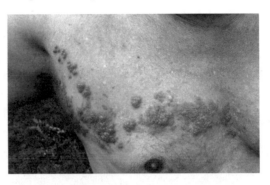

By Fisle - Own work, CC BY-SA 3.0, https://commons.wikimedia.org/w/index.php?curid=2558194

Therapeutic Management

1. Contact isolation or airborne isolation if disseminated rash
2. Assess neurological status and s/s infection
3. Medications→ Antivirals, NSAIDs, the shingles vaccine (prevention)

Pressure Ulcers

Overview

1. Ulcerations in the skin varying in size and depth
2. Due to the compression of tissue for an extended period of time

General

1. Stage I→ Skin intact, non-blanchable redness
2. Stage II→ Partial thickness loss of skin
3. Stage III→ Full-thickness skin loss extends to the dermis and SubQ tissue
4. Stage IV→ Full-thickness skin loss, muscle and bone undermining and tunneling, and eschar or slough may be present
5. Deep Tissue Injury→ Injury to SubQ tissue under intact skin, Dark purple or brown
6. Unstageable→ Wound completely covered by eschar or slough – unable visualize or determine depth/thickness

Image 6.75 Pressure Ulcer Staging

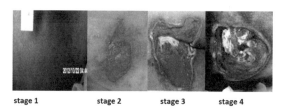

By Babagolzadeh - Own work, CC BY-SA 3.0, https://commons.wikimedia. org/w/index.php?curid=23432205

Image 6.76 Common Pressure Ulcer Sites

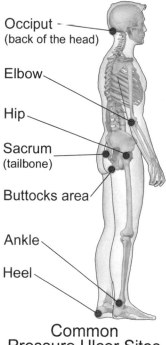

By BruceBlaus - Own work, CC BY-SA 4.0, https://commons.wikimedia. org/w/index.php?curid=61131815

Assessment

1. Check bony prominences with every turn. If redness present, press with finger to ensure blanching (turning white)
2. Albumin level to assess nutrition

Therapeutic Management

1. Consult Wound Care specialty nurse
2. Do NOT massage reddened area
3. Intervene as needed for malnutrition and immobility
4. Turn q2h or more often
5. Keep skin clean and dry
6. Minimize sheets under the client
7. Utilize specialty beds or surfaces
8. Offload bony prominences with pillow or wedge
9. Keep client's skin dry

Cheatsheet 6.22 Pressure Ulcer Staging

PRESSURE ULCERS

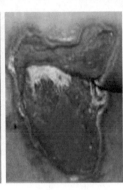
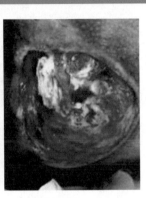

Stage 1   **Stage 2**   **Stage 3**   **Stage 4**

STAGING

Stage I	Intact skin with non-blanchable redness of a localized area usually over a bony prominence. Darkly pigmented skin may not have visible blanching; its color may differ from the surrounding area.
Stage II	Partial thickness loss of dermis presenting as a shallow open ulcer with a red pink wound bed, without slough. May also present as an intact or open/ruptured serum-filled blister. Presents as a shiny or dry shallow ulcer without slough or bruising.
Stage III	Full thickness tissue loss. Subcutaneous fat may be visible but bone, tendon or muscle are not exposed. Slough may be present but does not obscure the depth of tissue loss. May include undermining and tunneling.
Stage IV	Full thickness tissue loss with exposed bone, tendon or muscle. Slough or eschar may be present on some parts of the wound bed. Often include undermining and tunneling.
Unstageable	Full thickness tissue loss in which actual depth of the ulcer is completely obscured by slough (yellow, tan, gray, green or brown) and/or eschar (tan, brown or black) in the wound bed. Until enough slough and/or eschar is removed to expose the base of the wound, the true depth, and therefore stage, cannot be determined.
DTI	A purple or maroon localized area of discolored intact skin or blood-filled blister due to damage of underlying soft tissue from pressure and/or shear. The area may be preceded by tissue that is painful, firm, mushy, boggy, warmer or cooler as compared to adjacent tissue.

Treatment

- Identify at risk patients and institute precautions and assessments.
- Keep skin dry, sheets wrinkle free, turn and reposition frequently.
- Assess and document status of ulcer.
- Treatment may include creams, dressings, debridement, grafting, vacuum assisted suction.

Image Credit: By Babagolzadeh (Own work) [CC BY-SA 3.0 (http://creativecommons.org/licenses/by-sa/3.0)], via Wikimedia Commons

Addison's Disease

Overview

1. Hyposecretion of adrenal cortex hormones
2. Decreased levels of glucocorticoids and mineralocorticoids lead to electrolyte imbalances and decreased vascular volume

General

1. **Adrenal Cortex**
   a. Glucocorticoids (ie. cortisol) are in charge of glucose, fat metabolism, and anti-inflammatory
   b. Mineralocorticoids (ie. aldosterone) whose deficiency leads to hyponatremia, hyperkalemia
   c. Sex hormones (Androgens) i.e Testosterone, Estrogen which controls physical features and hair distribution
2. **Adrenal Medulla**
   a. Epinephrine (Adrenaline), Norepinephrine (Noradrenaline), Fight or Flight Response

Assessment

1. **Cardiovascular**
   a. Hypotension, tachycardia
2. **Metabolic**
   a. Weight loss
3. **Integumentary**
   a. Hyperpigmentation (bronzing)
4. **Electrolytes**
   a. Hyperkalemia, hypercalcemia, hyponatremia, and hypoglycemia
5. **Addisonian Crisis**
   a. Acute exacerbation
   b. Severe electrolyte disturbance

Therapeutic Management

1. **Replace adrenal hormones**
   a. Corticosteroids→ Hydrocortisone, prednisone
2. **Addisonian Crisis**
   a. Monitor electrolytes and cardiovascular status closely
   b. Administer adrenal hormones as ordered
   c. Administer electrolyte replacement as needed

Image 6.65 Addison's Disease

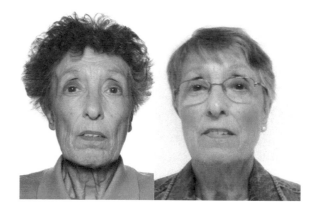

By Petros Perros - A 69-Year-Old Female with Tiredness and a Persistent Tan, CC BY 2.5, https://commons.wikimedia.org/w/index.php?curid=8256006

ADDISON'S VS. CUSHING'S

ADRENAL GLAND DISORDERS

The Adrenal Glands sit on top of the kidneys. The Adrenal Cortex secretes glucocorticoids, mineralocorticoids, and androgen hormones. Addison's and Cushing's Disease are conditions of either too little (hypo) or too much (hyper) secretion of hormones from the adrenal cortex.

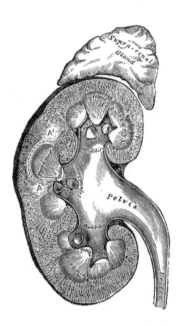

Body System	Addison's (Hypo)	Cushing's (Hyper)
Cardiovascular	Hypotension Tachycardia	Hypertension Volume Overload
Metabolic	Weight Loss	Moon Face Buffalo Hump
Integumentary	Hyperpigmentation (bronze skin)	Fragile Skin Striae on Abdomen
Electrolytes	Hypercalcemia Hypoglycemia Hyperkalemia Hyponatremia	Hypocalcemia Hyperglycemia Hypokalemia Hypernatremia

Cushing's Syndrome

Overview

Hypersecretion of glucocorticoids leading to elevated cortisol level

General

1. **Causes**
   a. Adrenal or pituitary tumor and the pituitary gland controls adrenal hormones
   b. Overuse or chronic use of corticosteroids
2. **Cushing's syndrome**
   a. Excess cortisol
   b. Excess aldosterone
   c. Excess androgens

Assessment

1. **Cardiovascular**→ Hypertension, signs of heart failure
2. **Metabolic**→ Redistribution of fats, moon face, and buffalo hump
3. **Integumentary**→ Excess hair, striae on the abdomen, fragile skin, and peripheral edema
4. **Electrolytes**→ Hypokalemia, hypocalcemia, hypernatremia, hyperglycemia
5. **Decreased Immune Response**

Therapeutic Management

1. Remove adrenal or pituitary tumor
2. Decrease dose or stop corticosteroid use
3. Monitor Electrolytes and Cardiovascular Status→ Replace electrolytes as needed
4. Safety → Protect from Injury
   a. Risk for Osteoporosis (hypocalcemia)
   b. Risk for Infection
   c. Risk for Skin breakdown

Image 6.66 Cushing's Syndrome Signs

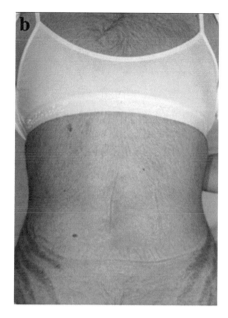

By Ozlem Celik, Mutlu Niyazoglu, Hikmet Soylu and Pinar Kadioglu - http://mrmjournal.biomedcentral.com/articles/10.1186/2049-6958-7-26, CC BY 2.5, https://commons.wikimedia.org/w/index.php?curid=47877334

Diabetic Ketoacidosis

General

1. Type I Diabetes Mellitus – Acute Exacerbation with severe Hyperglycemia with Ketoacidosis
   a. The body has NO insulin→ can't get glucose into cell → breaks down fatty acids for energy → Ketones (Acids)

Assessment

1. **Ketoacidosis**
   a. Acidosis (pH <7.35, HCO3- <22)
   b. Ketones in Urine
   c. Fruity Breath (due to ketones)
   d. Kussmaul Respirations
      i. Trying to breathe off CO_2 to compensate for acidosis
      ii. Clients can tire easily
   e. Hyperkalemia→ potassium leaves the cell to compensate for acidemia

2. **Hyperglycemia**
   a. Blood Glucose 400-600 mg/dL
   b. Severe Dehydration
      i. Osmotic Diuresis
      ii. Polyuria
   c. ↑ BUN, Creatinine
   d. Altered LOC (cellular dehydration)

Therapeutic Management

1. First nursing action = begin fluid replacement and check electrolytes
2. Treatment Priority = correct acidosis
   a. Insulin therapy → helps the body stop the breakdown of fatty acids
   b. Without insulin, DKA will continue to progress, despite the fluid replacement
   c. Insulin therapy continues until the anion gap acidosis has fully resolved
3. Continue replacing fluids as needed to help manage the dehydration caused by the hyperosmolarity
4. Monitor neurological status
5. Monitor and treat electrolyte imbalances

Cheatsheet 6.20 DKA vs HHNS

DKA vs HHNS

DKA: (Type I) hyperglycemic crisis associated with metabolic acidosis and elevated serum ketones.
HHNS: (Type II) hyperglycemic crisis with the absence of ketone formation.

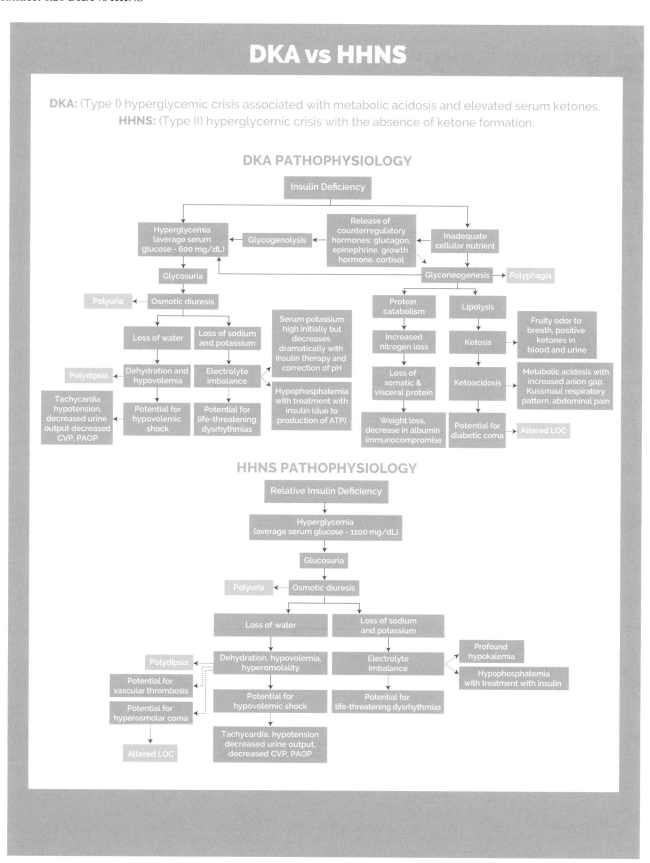

DKA PATHOPHYSIOLOGY

Insulin Deficiency

Hyperglycemia (average serum glucose - 600 mg/dL) ← Glycogenolysis ← Release of counterregulatory hormones: glucagon, epinephrine, growth hormone, cortisol → Inadequate cellular nutrient

Glycosuria → Glyconeogenesis → Polyphagia

Polyuria ← Osmotic diuresis

Protein catabolism — Lipolysis

Loss of water — Loss of sodium and potassium

Serum potassium high initially but decreases dramatically with insulin therapy and correction of pH

Fruity odor to breath, positive ketones in blood and urine

Increased nitrogen loss — Ketosis

Polydipsia ← Dehydration and hypovolemia — Electrolyte imbalance

Loss of somatic & visceral protein — Ketoacidosis

Metabolic acidosis with increased anion gap. Kussmaul respiratory pattern, abdominal pain

Hypophosphatemia with treatment with insulin (due to production of ATP)

Tachycardia hypotension, decreased urine output decreased CVP, PAOP

Potential for hypovolemic shock — Potential for life-threatening dysrhythmias

Weight loss, decrease in albumin immunocompromise — Potential for diabetic coma → Altered LOC

HHNS PATHOPHYSIOLOGY

Relative Insulin Deficiency

Hyperglycemia (average serum glucose - 1100 mg/dL)

Glucosuria

Polyuria ← Osmotic diuresis

Loss of water — Loss of sodium and potassium

Polydipsia ← Dehydration, hypovolemia, hyperomolality — Electrolyte imbalance → Profound hypokalemia / Hypophosphatemia with treatment with insulin

Potential for vascular thrombosis

Potential for hyperosmolar coma — Potential for hypovolemic shock — Potential for life-threatening dysrhythmias

Altered LOC — Tachycardia, hypotension decreased urine output, decreased CVP, PAOP

Diabetes Insipidus

Overview

Hyposecretion or failure to respond to antidiuretic hormone (ADH) from the posterior pituitary, which leads to excess water loss

General

1. Urine output → 4L to 30L in a 24 hour period
2. Excessive dehydration
3. Causes
   a. Neurogenic→ stroke, tumor
   b. Infection
   c. Pituitary surgery (pituitary gland secretes ADH)

Assessment

1. Polyuria → Excessive urine output→ dilute urine, Urine Specific Gravity <1.006
2. Polydipsia (extreme thirst)
3. Hypotension leading to cardiovascular collapse
4. Tachycardia
5. Hypernatremia, neurological changes

Therapeutic Management

1. Water replacement
   a. PO Free Water (plain water)
   b. D5W if IV replacement required
2. Hormone replacement→ DDAVP (Desmopressin/ Vasopressin) → Synthetic ADH
3. Monitor urine output hourly (Report UO >200mL/ hour), monitor urine specific gravity
4. Daily weight monitoring

Diabetes Mellitus

Overview

1. A pancreatic disorder resulting in insufficient or lack of insulin production leading to elevated blood sugar
2. Insulin is the "key" to allow glucose to enter cells and be used for energy

General

1. **Type I**
   a. Autoimmune disorder
   b. Body attacks beta cells in the pancreas (responsible for insulin production)
   c. The pancreas makes NO insulin, the client is insulin-dependent
   d. Ketosis due to gluconeogenesis (body making glucose from fat cells), since it can not use the glucose in the blood because the "key" is missing

2. **Type II**
   a. Beta cells do not produce enough insulin for the body's needs
   b. OR – Body becomes resistant to insulin
   c. Lifestyle-related
   d. May or may not require insulin, depending on the severity

Assessment

1. **Vascular and Nerve Damage**
   a. Related to inflammation and hyperosmolarity in vessels
   b. Poor circulation→ because the blood is thick with glucose
   c. Poor wound healing
   d. Retinopathy → blurry vision
   e. Neuropathy → decreased sensation, especially in feet/toes
   f. Nephropathy → may result in Chronic Kidney Disease

2. **The Three P's**
   a. Polyuria
   b. Polydipsia
   c. Polyphagia

3. **Elevated HgbA1c > 7.0**
   a. A measure of the average blood sugar over the last 3 months

4. **Complications**
   a. Dawn Phenomenon→ Reduced insulin sensitivity between 5-8am that can be helped with evening insulin administration
   b. Somogyi Phenomenon→ Nighttime hypoglycemia results in rebound hyperglycemia in the morning hours, which can be helped with a bedtime snack
   c. Diabetic Ketoacidosis (DKA) → Acute exacerbation of Type I Diabetes Mellitus (hyperglycemia resulting in the spilling of sugar into the urine)
   d. Hyperglycemic Hyperosmolar Nonketotic State (HHNS) → Acute exacerbation of Type II Diabetes Mellitus (Caused by increased blood sugar levels which leads to ↑ osmotic pressure in vessels → cellular dehydration)

Image 6.68 Symptoms of Diabetes Mellitus

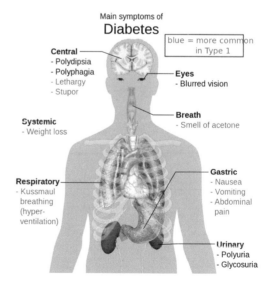

Therapeutic Management

1. **Oral Antidiabetic Agents**
   a. For Type II Diabetics
   b. Glucophage (Metformin) = most common
   c. Glipizide (Glucotrol)

2. **Insulin**
   a. Required for Type I
   b. Type II may require insulin if diet, exercise, and oral antidiabetic agents aren't enough
   c. Most at risk for hypoglycemia during insulin peak times
   d. ONLY Regular insulin can be given by IV
   e. Mixing Regular and NPH
      i. Clear before Cloudy
      ii. Inject the air into cloudy → Inject the air into clear and draw up clear → draw up cloudy
      iii. Avoids cross-contamination or errors in drawing up
   f. "Insulin Reaction" → hypoglycemia
      i. Cool, clammy, diaphoretic
      ii. 15-15 Rule: Give 15 g sugar (4 oz. juice or soda) and recheck in 15 minutes

3. **Diet and Exercise**
   a. May improve insulin response for Type II Diabetics AND can help stabilize blood sugars in Type I Diabetics.

Hyperglycemic Hyperosmolar Nonketotic Syndrome (HHNS)

Image 6.69 Priority Fluid Replacement for DKA/HHNS

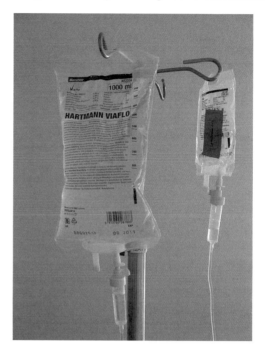

General

1. Type II Diabetes Mellitus – Acute Exacerbation
   a. The body has just enough insulin to prevent fatty acid breakdown, but there is severe hyperglycemia without ketoacidosis

Assessment

1. **Hyperglycemia**
   a. Blood sugar > 600 mg/dL (usually higher)
   b. Negative Ketones
   c. Glycosuria (glucose dumps in urine)
2. **Hyperosmolarity**
   a. PROFOUND Dehydration
   b. Altered LOC
   c. Dry mucous membranes
   d. ↑ BUN, Creatinine

Therapeutic Management

1. Identify and treat the cause
2. #1 Priority = replace fluids, which MIGHT RESOLVE the hyperglycemia as well
3. Insulin Therapy
4. Monitor neurological status
5. Monitor and treat electrolyte imbalances

Hyperthyroidism

Overview

1. Excess secretion of thyroid hormone (TH) from thyroid gland
2. Results in Increased Metabolic Rate

General

1. **Causes**
   a. Graves Disease (autoimmune)
   b. Excess secretion of TSH from Pituitary
   c. Thyroid, Pituitary, or Hypothalamic Tumor
   d. Medication Reaction
2. **Thyroid Storm (Thyroid Crisis)**
   a. Acute Exacerbation due to infection, stress, trauma

Assessment

1. **Hormone changes**
   a. ↑ T3, T4, Free T4 hormones
   b. ↓ TSH
2. **Positive radioactive iodine uptake scan**
3. **Possible presence of a goiter**
4. **Cardiac changes**
   a. Tachycardia, HTN, palpitations
5. **Neurological changes**
   a. Hyperactive reflexes, hand tremor
   b. Emotional instability, agitation
6. **Sensory changes**
   a. Exophthalmos (bulging eyes)
   b. Blurred vision
7. **Integumentary changes**
   a. Fine, thin hair
8. **Reproductive changes**
   a. Amenorrhea
   b. Change in Libido
      i. Some clients experience increased libido, while others report decreased libido

9. **Metabolic changes**
   a. Hypermetabolic
   b. ↑ Temperature
   c. Heat intolerance
   d. Weight Loss
   e. Hypocalcemia
      i. Due to excess Calcitonin
10. **Thyroid Storm (Thyroid Crisis)**
    a. Febrile state
    b. Tachycardia, HTN
    c. Tremors
    d. Seizures

Therapeutic Management

1. **Provide rest in a cool, quiet environment**
2. **Cardiac monitoring as ordered**
3. **Maintain patent airway**
4. **Provide eye protection for exophthalmos**
   a. Regular eye exams
   b. Eye drops for moisture
5. **Medications**
   a. Antithyroid medications → propylthiouracil or methimazole
   b. Radioactive Iodine 131 → taken up by thyroid gland
      i. Destroys some thyroid cells over 6-8 weeks
      ii. Avoid in pregnancy
      iii. Monitor for hypothyroidism
6. **Surgical Removal of Thyroid (Thyroidectomy)**
   a. Monitor airway (swelling)
      i. Assess for obstruction, stridor, dysphagia
      ii. Have tracheotomy equipment available
   b. Maintain upright position
   c. Assess for bleeding
   d. Monitor for hypocalcemia
      i. Removal of the parathyroid glands causes a decrease in (parathyroid hormone), which helps to maintain blood calcium levels.
2. Have calcium gluconate available PRN
   e. Minimal talking after surgery

Hypothyroidism

Overview

Hyposecretion of thyroid hormone that results in a decreased metabolic rate

General

1. **Causes**
   a. Hashimoto's Thyroiditis
   b. Iodine Deficiency
   c. Thyroidectomy
2. Myxedema Coma
   a. Acute Exacerbation
   b. Life-threatening state of decreased thyroid production
   c. Caused by acute illness, rapid cessation of medication, or hypothermia

Assessment

1. Hypometabolic state
2. Goiter – enlarged thyroid due to iodine deficiency
3. ↓ T3, T4, Free T4 hormones
4. ↑ TSH levels
5. Cardiovascular→ Bradycardia, hypotension, anemia
6. Gastrointestinal→ Constipation
7. Neurological→ Lethargy, fatigue, weakness
8. Integumentary→ Dry skin, loss of body hair
9. Metabolic→ Cold intolerance, anorexia, weight gain, edema, hypoglycemia

Image 6.67 Symptoms of Hypothyroidism

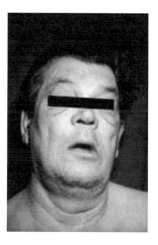

By Herbert L. Fred, MD and Hendrik A. van Dijk - http://cnx.org/content/m15004/latest/, CC BY 2.5, https://commons.wikimedia.org/w/index.php?curid=30826141

Therapeutic Management

1. Medication Therapy
   a. Levothyroxine (Synthroid)
   b. Monitor – possible overdose
2. Cardiac Monitoring
3. Maintain open airway, especially with goiter→ Have tracheotomy supplies available
4. IV fluids to support hemodynamics
5. Administer glucose/dextrose as needed
6. Encourage nutrition intake
7. Assess thyroid hormone levels

SIADH (Syndrome of Inappropriate Antidiuretic Hormone)

Overview

1. Excess secretion of ADH from the posterior pituitary
2. Hyponatremia (excess water diluting sodium)
3. Water intoxication

Assessment

1. Fluid Volume Excess→ Hypertension, JVD, Crackles
2. Hyponatremia → Altered LOC, coma, seizures
3. Concentrated Urine→ Decreased urine output, urine Specific Gravity > 1.036
4. Diluted blood circulation so decreased BUN, decreased Hematocrit

Therapeutic Management

1. Frequent cardiac monitoring
2. Frequent neurological examination
3. Monitor I&O and fluid restriction
4. Daily weight
5. Sodium supplement
6. Medication→ Hypertonic saline, diuretics, electrolyte replacement

🧑‍⚕️ Fractures

General

1. **Types of fractures**
   a. *Closed* – skin intact
   b. *Open/Compound* – bone pierces the skin
   c. *Transverse* – broken straight across
   d. *Spiral* – fracture from twisting force
   e. *Comminuted* – multiple pieces of bone
   f. *Impacted* – from the vertical force on long bone
   g. *Greenstick* – incomplete fracture, common in children
   h. *Oblique* – diagonal fracture
   i. *Displaced* – bones no longer aligned

2. **Strain**
   a. Excessive stretching of the muscle

3. **Sprain**
   a. Excessive stretching of a ligament

4. **Complications**
   a. Fat Embolism (when a piece of fat from bone marrow moves through the bloodstream to lungs) is a risk with long-bone fractures.
   b. Compartment Syndrome is when increased pressure within the compartment in the extremity after a fracture or crush injury cuts off circulation to muscles and nerves

Assessment

1. **Fracture**
   a. Assess distal circulation→ Pulses, skin temperature, color
   b. Assess distal nerve function→ Numbness and tingling
   c. May see ecchymosis over the fractured area

2. **Fat Embolism**
   a. Anxiety, restlessness
   b. Tachycardia, hypotension
   c. Tachypnea, dyspnea
   d. Petechial rash

3. **Compartment Syndrome**
   a. Pale skin
   b. Extreme swelling
   c. Loss of pulses or sensation distal to the injury

Image 6.86 Fractures

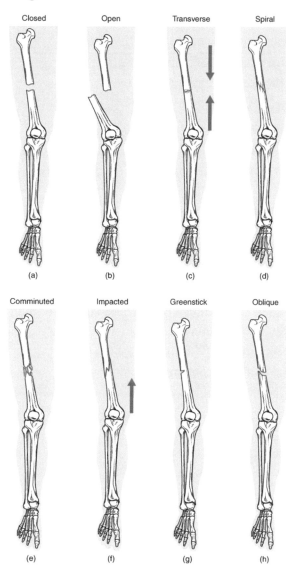

By OpenStax College - Anatomy & Physiology, Connexions Web site. http://cnx.org/content/col11496/1.6/, Sep 7, 2015., CC BY 4.0, https://commons.wikimedia.org/w/index.php?curid=30127535

Therapeutic Management

1. **RICE**
   a. Rest
   b. Ice
   c. Compression
   d. Elevation

2. **Cast**
   a. Stabilization of bone for healing.
   b. Monitor extremity for:
      i. Swelling
      ii. Pain
      iii. Discoloration
      iv. Sensation
      v. Circulation distal to cast

3. **Traction**
   a. Force applied in the opposite direction to realign and immobilize the fracture
   b. Ensure proper alignment of the body
   c. Buck's Traction – force applied to splint
   d. Skeletal Traction – pin inserted through bone to hold traction force
   e. Weights should hang freely from bed
      i. Do not set them on the floor
      ii. Do not remove weights without provider order
      iii. Support weight when sliding up in bed

4. **Fat Embolism**
   a. No specific treatment
   b. Support hemodynamics
   c. Corticosteroids
   d. Monitor in ICU

5. **Compartment Syndrome**
   a. Emergent intervention required to prevent loss of limb
   b. Fasciotomy required to relieve pressure

Osteoporosis

Overview

Bone demineralization leading to a decrease in bone mass/density

General

1. Bone resorption occurs faster than formation leading to Ca loss from bones and ↓ bone density
   a. Possible Calcium or Vitamin D absorption issues
2. More common in post-menopausal due to ↓ estrogen
3. Can be caused by steroid use because this increases the bone resorption rate

Assessment

1. ↓ Dietary Ca+ intake
2. Kyphosis of spine
3. Bone pain
4. Fractures of pelvic or hip
5. Pathological fractures are those that occur without trauma.

Therapeutic Management

1. Ca+ intake and supplementation
2. Vitamin D intake because vitamin D is necessary for the absorption of Ca+
3. Weight-bearing exercises (PT/OT)
4. Medications→ should be taken 30 minutes prior to eating ie. Alendronate (Fosamax)/Risedronate (Actonel)

Image 6.85 Osteoporosis

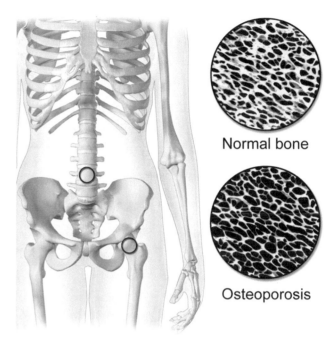

By BruceBlaus - Own work, CC BY-SA 4.0, https://commons.wikimedia.org/w/index.php?curid=46602308

Parkinson's Disease

Overview

1. Degenerative neurological disorder
2. Atrophy of substantia nigra → depletion of dopamine→ Less and less capable of controlled movement

Image 6.39 Parkinsons Pathophysiology

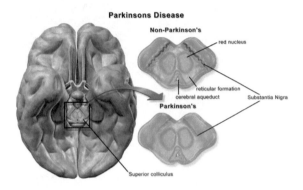

Blausen.com staff (2014). "Medical gallery of Blausen Medical 2014". WikiJournal of Medicine 1 (2). DOI:10.15347/wjm/2014.010. ISSN 2002-4436. - Own work, CC BY 3.0, https://commons.wikimedia.org/w/index.php?curid=27924394

General

1. Slow, progressive disease, no cure
2. Progressively debilitated and self-care dependent

Assessment

1. **Classic Signs:**
   a. Pill rolling – tremors in hands (as if rolling a pill between fingers)
   b. Shuffling Gait
   c. Lip Smacking
   d. Bradykinesia – slow movements due to muscle rigidity
   e. Resting tremor
   f. Akinesia → loss of voluntary movement
   g. Blank facial expression
   h. Stooped stance
   i. Drooling
   j. Dysphagia

Therapeutic Management

1. **Medication therapy**
   a. Dopaminergic
   b. Dopamine agonists→ Levodopa-Carbidopa
   c. Anticholinergics
2. **The goal is to increase the levels of available dopamine in the CNS**

Ischemic Stroke

Overview

Lack of blood flow to brain tissue caused by a blood clot in the cerebral vessels.

General

1. **Pathophysiology**
   a. A blood clot in a vessel in the brain
   b. No flow past clot
   c. Not immediately seen on CT scan (24 hours), MRI for a better view
2. **Presentation dependent on the location of the clot**
   a. MCA – classic FAST symptoms → contralateral manifestations
   b. Basilar – decreased LOC, loss of vision, abnormal pupil response
   c. Brainstem – loss of BP regulation, Respiratory Failure, dysphagia

Image 6.41 Ischemic Stroke

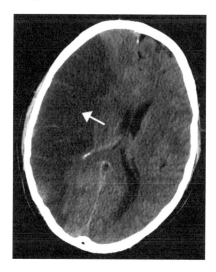

By INFARCT.jpg: Lucien Monfilsderivative work: Suraj - INFARCT. jpg, CC BY-SA 3.0, https://commons.wikimedia.org/w/index. php?curid=16444670

Multiple Sclerosis

Overview

1. Chronic, progressive demyelination of neurons in the CNS
2. Memory Aid: Multiple Sclerosis → Myelin Sheath

Assessment

1. Fatigue
2. Tremors
3. Weakness
4. Spasticity of muscles→ Can be painful
5. Bowel and Bladder dysfunction→ Incontinence, diarrhea, or constipation
6. Decreased peripheral sensation (pain, temperature, touch) → High risk for injury
7. Visual disturbances
8. Emotional instability

Image 6.38 Multiple Sclerosis Symptoms

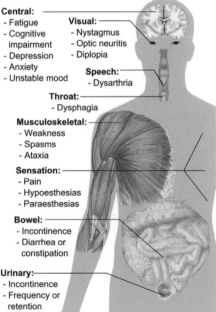

Therapeutic Management

1. No cure → supportive therapy, analgesics, muscle relaxants
2. Energy conservation
3. Provide bowel and bladder training
4. Maintain adequate fluid intake of 2000 mL/day
5. Encourage activity independence
6. Regulate temperatures on water heaters, baths, and heating pads→ Risk for burns
7. Ensure in-home safety (rugs, cords, etc) → Risk for falls

⚠ Hemorrhagic Stroke

General

1. **Pathophysiology**
   a. Bleed in/around the brain due to ruptured vessel
   b. Hypertension → weakened vessel (i.e. aneurysm rupture) No flow past point of bleed
   c. Visible immediately on CT scan
   d. Presents as "worst headache of my life" (especially Subarachnoid Hemorrhage)

2. **Risk Factors**
   a. Hypertension, substance abuse (cocaine), anticoagulant therapy, trauma

3. **Complications**
   a. Blood = irritant to tissues
   b. Seizures
   c. Vasospasm – vessels clampdown→ Cause more ischemia

Image 6.40 Hemorrhagic Stroke

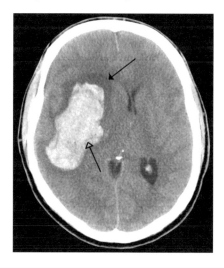

By James Heilman, MD - Own work, CC BY-SA 3.0, https://commons.wikimedia.org/w/index.php?curid=16263217

Meningitis

Overview

Inflammation of the membranes around the brain and spinal cord caused by a virus, bacteria, fungus, or protozoa

General

1. **CSF is analyzed to determine diagnosis**
   a. Cloudy
   b. ↑ WBC
   c. ↓ Glucose

Assessment

1. **Fever**
2. **Altered level of consciousness**
3. **Nuchal rigidity**
   a. Kernig's sign→ Severe stiffness of the hamstrings causes an inability to straighten the leg when the hip is flexed to a 90-degree angle
   b. Brudzinski's sign → Severe neck stiffness causes a client's hips and knees to flex when the neck is flexed.
4. **Lethargy**
5. **Increased Intracranial Pressure**
6. **Photophobia**
7. **Seizures**

Therapeutic Management

1. **Place in droplet isolation**
2. **Analgesics**
3. **Antibiotics**
   a. Consider Blood-Brain-Barrier

Seizure Causes

Overview

1. **Abrupt, abnormal, excessive, uncontrolled electrical activity in neurons of the brain**
2. **Types**
   a. *Generalized – both hemispheres*
      i. Tonic-clonic→ Stiffening (contraction), jerking/twitching, and loss of consciousness
      ii. Absence→ staring off into space, unaware of surroundings, lasts <30 seconds
      iii. Tonic – Contraction/Tensing of muscles
      iv. Clonic – Jerking/Twitching
      v. Myoclonic – sudden jerk of muscles
      vi. Atonic→ All muscles suddenly go limp (High fall risk)
   b. *Focal – Localized – one hemisphere*
      i. Simple→ Twitching or sensory changes, client remains conscious
      ii. Complex→ Twitching or outbursts (laugh or cry), loss of consciousness/awareness
3. **Status epilepticus**
   a. A persistent seizure with no breaks between episodes and a *MEDICAL EMERGENCY*

 # Seizure Assessment

Assessment

1. Before Seizure→ assess risk factors for medication compliance and assess for Aura, which is a sensation that warns of impending seizure
   i. Different for every client→ Some see colors, smell metal, or feel tingly
2. During a seizure, assess and document the type, onset, duration, and complications (biting tongue, aspiration, or injury)
3. Postictal State → period AFTER seizure where there is some memory loss, sleepiness, impaired speech, disorientation, agitation

Image 6.42 Generalized Seizure

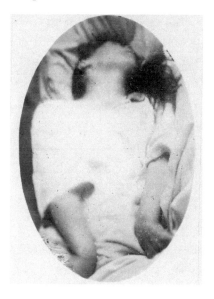

 # Seizure Therapeutic Management

Overview

1. **EEG Diagnostics**
   a. Tests types of brainwaves where seizures are occurring and the severity
2. **Medications**
   a. Antiepileptic drug→ Stop seizures:
      1. Lorazepam (Ativan) → First-line drug, 2 mg IV push during seizure
      2. Diazepam (Valium)
      3. Phenobarbital
   b. Prevent seizures → Phenytoin (Dilantin), Fosphenytoin (Cerebyx), Levetiracetam (Keppra), Lacosamide (Vimpat)
3. **Procedures**
   a. Surgical removal of lesion
   b. Cutting connections in brain
   c. Deep Brain Stimulation
      i. Corpus callosotomy surgery
      ii. Extratemporal resection

Seizure Nursing Care

Overview

1. **Before**
   a. Give all medications on time
   b. Seizure precautions if at risk
   c. Verify order of PRN dosing and ensure that medication is readily available.

2. **During**
   a. Maintain client airway
      i. Turn client to side in case of vomit
      ii. Have oxygen and suction equipment available
      iii. DO NOT force anything into the mouth during a seizure (including bite block)
   b. Protect from injury
      i. Bed to the lowest position
      ii. Padded side rails
      iii. Loosen restrictive clothing
      iv. DO NOT try to restrain the client
   c. Notify MD of type, onset, duration

3. **After**
   a. Keep safe while Postictal

Intracranial Pressure ICP

Overview

1. **Intracranial Pressure**
   a. Pressure within the cranium
   b. Normal = 5-15 mmHg
   c. Intervention required at >20 mmHg

General

1. **Causes**
   a. Tumor or mass
   b. Bleeding from stroke or trauma
   c. Hydrocephalus
   d. Trauma → edema
   e. Ischemic stroke → edema
2. **Brain Herniation**
   a. ICP increases to the point that brain tissue squeezes through/across a structure in the skull→ Permanent Damage can lead to brain death

Assessment

1. **Altered LOC**
   a. Confusion
   b. Stupor
   c. May be subtle
2. **Pupillary changes**
   a. Fixed and dilated indicates prolonged increased ICP
3. **Babinski Reflex**
   a. Positive response= bad
4. **Posturing**
5. **Seizures**
6. **Cushing's Triad** → impending herniation
   a. Abnormal respirations
   b. Widened pulse pressure
   c. Bradycardia
7. **Elevated Temp (loss of regulation)**

Therapeutic Management

1. Avoid sedative or CNS depressant
2. Hyperventilation → "Permissive Hypocapnia" for cerebral vasoconstriction
3. Osmotic Diuretics → Mannitol to decrease swelling
4. Hypertonic Saline (1.5% or 3%) to decrease swelling
5. Corticosteroids to decrease inflammation
6. Craniectomy (AKA "Bone Flap") to make room for the brain to swell
7. External Ventricular Drain (AKA "EVD" "Bolt) to drains CSF when ICP elevated
   a. A "Bolt" is only capable of measuring intracranial pressures
   b. EVD is able to measure pressure and drain CSF through the ventriculostomy

Routine Neuro Assessments

Assessment

1. **Level of Consciousness**
   a. Assess alertness
   b. Assess orientation, Person, place, time, situation
   c. Assess response to stimuli
      i. Start with verbal
      ii. Then light touch
      iii. Deep touch/shaking
      iv. Painful (nail beds)
      v. Deep pain (sternal rub)

2. **Glasgow Coma Scale**
   a. Can never be zero (0)
   b. Worst score is 3, with best being 15
   c. In each category, give the highest score, and then add all three scores up
      i. *Best Eye Opening*
         1. 4 – spontaneous
         2. 3 – to voice
         3. 2 – to pain
         4. 1 – no response
      ii. *Best Verbal Response*
         1. 5 – oriented
         2. 4 – disoriented, converses
         3. 3 – inappropriate words
         4. 2 – incomprehensible speech
         5. 1 – no response / intubated
      iii. *Best Motor Response*
         1. 6 – follows commands
         2. 5 – localizes to pain (when pain response initiated, client reaches toward pain)
         3. 4 – withdraws from pain (when pain response initiated, client reaches toward pain, but cannot cross the midline, or the middle, of the body)
         4. 3 – abnormal flexion ("decorticate")
         5. 2 – abnormal extension ("decerebrate")
         6. 1 – no movement
   d. Example:
      i. A client who opens their eyes to voice (3), is disoriented (4) and follows commands (6) can be given a GCS of 13.
      ii. A client who does not open their eyes (1), does not respond verbally (1) and who is decorticate (3) receives a GCS of 5.

3. **Pupil Assessment**
   a. Equal, Round, Size
   b. Reactive to Light→ Should constrict briskly, and equally on both sides when the light shined in eyes
   c. Accommodation→ Should constrict when focusing from far to near

Image 6.34 Normal Pupils

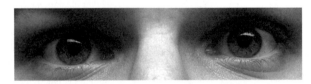

By Guy91 at the English language Wikipedia, CC BY-SA 3.0, https://commons.wikimedia.org/w/index.php?curid=16644397

Image 6.35 Constricted Pupils

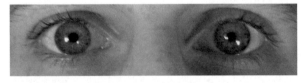

By Anonymous - Anonymous, CC0, https://commons.wikimedia.org/w/index.php?curid=22179521

Image 6.36 Unequal Pupils

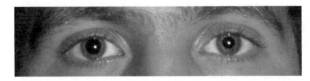

By Radomil talk - Own work, CC BY-SA 3.0, https://commons.wikimedia.org/w/index.php?curid=1348100

Image 6.37 Dilated Pupils

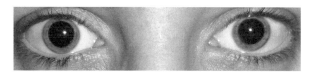

By Ilovebaddies (talk) - Own work., CC BY-SA 3.0, https://en.wikipedia.
org/w/index.php?curid=33000944

4. **Strength x 4 Extremities**
   a. 5 – full strength
   b. 4 – overcomes some resistance
   c. 3 – overcomes gravity, no resistance
   d. 2 – cannot overcome gravity
   e. 1 – no movement at all

Therapeutic Management

1. Notify provider of any acute changes
2. May need STAT CT or MRI to rule out possible increased intracranial pressure or stroke

Cheatsheet 6.9 Routine Neuro Assessments

ROUTINE NEURO ASSESSMENTS

Pupils Equal, Round, and Reactive to Light and Accommodation (PERRLA) + Size in mm

1mm 2mm 3mm 4mm 5mm 6mm 8mm

LEVELS OF CONSCIOUSNESS

Normal	A&O x 4, Alert
Confused	A&O x <3, unable to answer
Delirious	Confused and agitated
Somnolent	Excessively sleepy or drowsy
Obtunded	Awake, but slow or no response to surroundings
Stuporous	Sleep-like, no spontaneous activity, withdraws to pain
Coma	NO response to stimuli, unable to arouse

GLASGOW COMA SCALE

SCORE	1	2	3	4	5	6
Eyes	No opening	Open to pain	Open to voice	Open spontaneously	-	-
Verbal	No response	Incomprehensible sounds	Inappropriate words	Disoriented	Oriented	-
Motor	No response	Abnormal Extension	Abnormal Flexion	Withdraws to Pain	Localizes to Pain	Follows Commands

MUSCLE STRENGTH

SCORE	ABILITY
0	No muscle contraction
1	Muscle twitch
2	Movement without gravity
3	Movement against gravity
4	Movement against resistance
5	Full Strength

Alveoli & Atelectasis

Overview

Atelectasis is the collapse of a lung or lung lobe due to the deflating of the alveoli

General

1. Alveoli deflate, Collapse of the lung
2. Common after surgery→ Shallow breathing
3. Excessive pulmonary secretions

Assessment

1. Diminished breath sounds on the affected side
2. Chest pain with breathing
3. Fever
4. Chest X-ray shows collapse (white)

Therapeutic Management

1. *CPT (Chest Physiotherapy)* → Vibrations to loosen secretions
2. *IPPB (Intermittent Positive Pressure Breathing)* → Positive pressure to open alveoli
3. *IS (Incentive Spirometer)* – Slow deep breaths
   a. ↑ volume = reinflate alveoli
4. *Position Changes*→ Mobilize secretions
5. *Invasive Mechanical Ventilation*

Image 6.23 Atelectasis

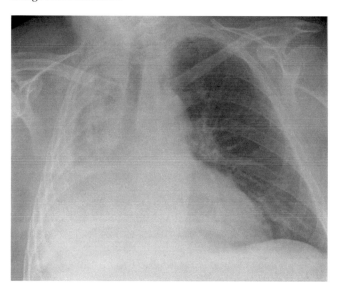

By The original uploader was Pabloes at Spanish Wikipedia - Transferred from es.wikipedia to Commons., CC BY-SA 3.0, https://commons.wikimedia.org/w/index.php?curid=1753377

Chronic Obstructive Pulmonary Disease - COPD

Overview

Chronic obstruction of airflow due to emphysema and chronic bronchitis

General

1. **Emphysema**
   a. Destruction of alveoli due to chronic inflammation
   b. Decreased surface area for gas exchange
2. **Chronic Bronchitis**
   a. Chronic airway inflammation with productive cough
   b. Excessive sputum production

Assessment

1. **Barrel chest**
   a. Expanded rib cage due to increased work when breathing and air trapping
2. **Accessory muscle use**
3. **Adventitious breath sounds**
   a. Diminished
   b. Crackles
   c. Wheezes
4. **Congestion on Chest X-ray**
5. **ABG → ↓ pH, ↑ pCO2, ↓ PaO2**

Therapeutic Management

1. **Do NOT give O2 > 2 Lpm**
   a. A stimulus to breathe = ↓ O2
2. **Chest Physiotherapy (CPT)**
   a. Loosen secretions
3. **Increase fluid intake (3 L / day) → Thin secretions**
4. **Medications→ Bronchodilators, corticosteroids**

Image 6.25 COPD

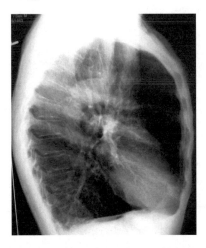

By James Heilman, MD - Own work, CC BY-SA 3.0, https://commons. wikimedia.org/w/index.php?curid=9500331

Asthma

Overview

1. Inflammatory disorder of airways
2. Stimulated by triggers (infection, allergens, exercise, irritants)
3. Status Asthmaticus – a life-threatening condition→ Asthma unresponsive to treatment

Assessment

1. **Symptoms**
   a. Narrowed airways→ Wheezing/crackles
   b. ↓ gas exchange→ Restless/anxious
   c. Inflammation of airways→ Diminished breath sounds and tachypnea

2. **Diagnostics**
   a. Peak Flow Rate
      i. The volume of expired air
      ii. Stable = 80-100% baseline
      iii. Caution = 50-80% baseline
      iv. Danger = <50% baseline
   b. Pulmonary Function Tests

Therapeutic Management

1. **High-Fowler's or position of comfort**
2. **Administer O2**
3. **Medications**
   a. Bronchodilators
   b. Corticosteroids
   c. Leukotriene Modulators (Montelukast/Singulair)

Image 6.24 Asthma

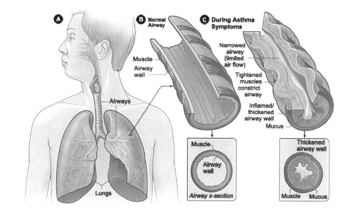

Artificial Airways

General

1. **Purpose**
   a. Protect airway when the client can't
   b. Provide route for mechanical ventilation

Assessment

1. Assess Airway
2. Assess Breathing
3. Assess Level of Consciousness
4. Choose correct airway
5. Call for help for advanced airway

Therapeutic Management

1. **Nasopharyngeal Airway**
   a. AKA "Nasal Trumpet"
   b. Client's can't clear secretions
   c. Breathing independently
   d. Conscious
2. **Oropharyngeal Airway**
   a. AKA "Oral Airway"
   b. Client can't protect airway
   c. Unconscious
3. **Endotracheal Tube**
   a. AKA "ET Tube" / "intubation"
   b. Client can't protect airway
   c. Not breathing or requires ventilation
   d. May be conscious or unconscious before intubation
4. **Tracheostomy Tube**
   a. AKA "Trach"
   b. Client has to be "weaned" (discontinued) from the ventilator slowly
   c. Long term requirement for the following:
   d. Neuromuscular
   e. Tracheal damage

Image 6.30 Tracheostomy

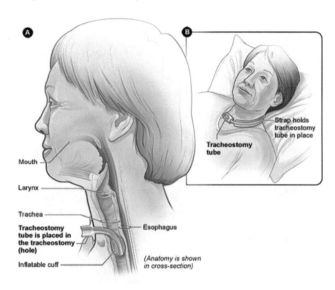

Image 6.31 Endotracheal Tube

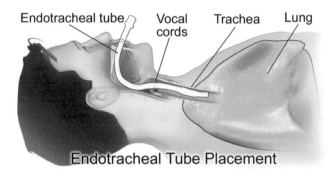

By BruceBlaus - Own work, CC BY-SA 4.0, https://commons.wikimedia.org/w/index.php?curid=57493229

Cheatsheet 6.8 Artificial Airways Decision Tree

ARTIFICIAL AIRWAYS DECISION TREE

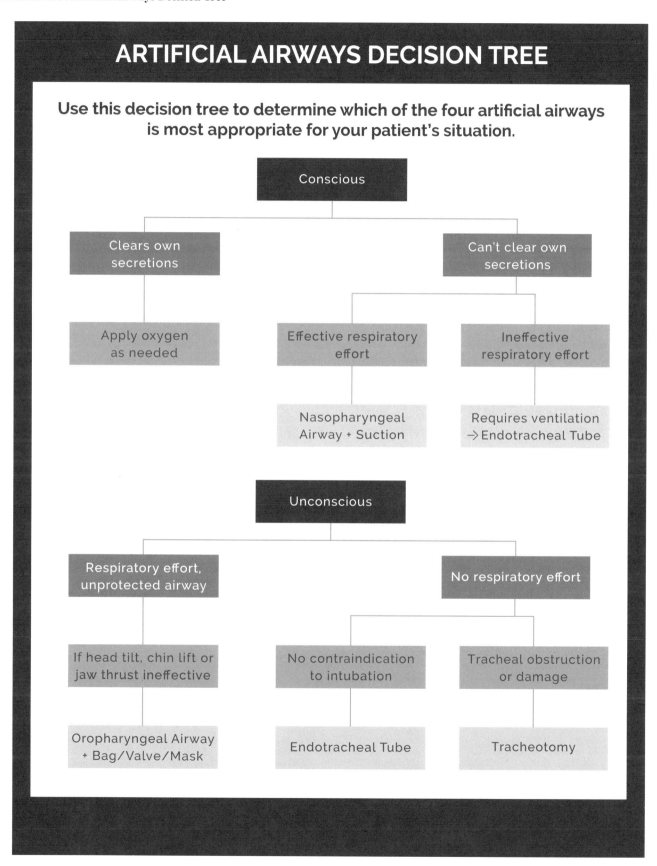

Use this decision tree to determine which of the four artificial airways is most appropriate for your patient's situation.

Conscious
- Clears own secretions → Apply oxygen as needed
- Can't clear own secretions
  - Effective respiratory effort → Nasopharyngeal Airway + Suction
  - Ineffective respiratory effort → Requires ventilation → Endotracheal Tube

Unconscious
- Respiratory effort, unprotected airway → If head tilt, chin lift or jaw thrust ineffective → Oropharyngeal Airway + Bag/Valve/Mask
- No respiratory effort
  - No contraindication to intubation → Endotracheal Tube
  - Tracheal obstruction or damage → Tracheotomy

Tuberculosis

Overview

1. Lung infection → pneumonitis and granulomas
2. Noncompliance → multi-drug resistance (MDR-TB)
3. Airborne transmission (infectious particles aerosolized)

General

1. **Risk Factors**
   a. Foreign travel
   b. Living in tight quarters→ College, prison, homeless Shelters
2. **Diagnostics**
   a. Chest X-ray shows granulomas
   b. TB Skin Test
      i. Anyone → 15 mm induration
      ii. High Risk → 10 mm induration
      iii. Immunocompromised → 5 mm induration
   c. Quantiferon Gold (gold standard)
   d. Sputum Cultures
      i. Mycobacterium tuberculosis

Assessment

1. **Night sweats**
2. **Weight Loss**
3. **Chills**
4. **Fatigue**
5. **Persistent cough**→ Hemoptysis (coughing up blood)
6. **Chest Pain**
7. **Anorexia**

Therapeutic Management

1. **Negative Pressure Room**
   a. RIPE Therapy:
      i. Rifampin
      ii. Isoniazid
      iii. Pyrazinamide
      iv. Ethambutol
   b. Treatment for 6-12 months→ Risk of transmission reduced after 2-3 weeks of medication regimen

Pneumonia

Overview

1. Inflammatory condition of the lungs
2. Primarily affecting the alveoli→ May fill with fluid or pus
3. Infectious vs Noninfectious
   a. Infectious→ Bacterial, Viral
   b. Non-infectious→ Aspiration

General

1. **Diagnosis**
   a. Chest X-ray
   b. Sputum culture to identify the organism

Assessment

1. **Viral**
   a. Low-grade fever
   b. Nonproductive cough
   c. WBCs normal to low elevation
   d. Chest X-ray shows minimal changes
   e. Less severe than bacterial
2. **Bacterial**
   a. High fever
   b. Productive cough
   c. WBCs elevated
   d. Chest X-ray shows infiltrate
   e. More severe than viral
3. **Both**
   a. Chills
   b. Rhonchi/Wheezes
   c. Sputum production

Therapeutic Management

1. **Medications**
   a. Antibiotics
   b. Analgesics
   c. Antipyretics
2. **Supplemental O2**
3. **Assess and maintain the respiratory status**
4. **Encourage activity as soon as possible**
5. **Instruct on chest expansion exercises→ Incentive spirometry, turn, cough, deep breathe**
6. **Encourage 3 L/day of fluids unless contraindicated→ Thin secretions**

Influenza

Overview

Influenza = virus (multiple strains), increasing severity→ Spread through droplet contact

Assessment

1. **Symptoms**
   a. Sudden onset
   b. Last 6-7 days
   c. Aches – head, muscles, body
   d. Fatigue
   e. Runny nose, sore throat, cough
   f. Vomiting
   g. High fever (102-104°F)

Image 6.26 Influenza Symptoms

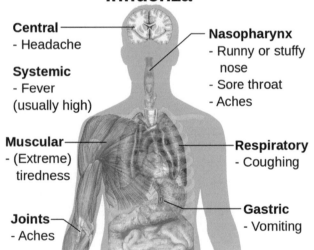

Therapeutic Management

1. **Vaccine**
   a. Indicated annually for:
      i. Healthcare workers
      ii. Elderly
      iii. Children > 6 mo
      iv. Pregnant
      v. Immunocompromised→ do NOT give immunocompromised clients the nasal spray vaccine
   b. Contraindications:
      i. Severe allergy to the flu vaccine, eggs, or latex
      ii. History of Guillain-Barre
      iii. Recent bone marrow or organ transplant (< 6 mo)
2. **Anti-Virals**
   a. Oseltamivir (Tamiflu)
      i. Within 48 hours of onset, best within 24 hours

Cognitive Impairment Disorders

Overview

Includes Autism-spectrum disorder (ASD), attention-deficit hyperactivity disorder (ADHD), Dementia, Alzheimer's Disease

General

1. **Dementia**
   a. A broad category of brain diseases that are gradual and long-term which result in self-care deficits, largely affecting a client's ability to function.
      i. Various types can affect people of varying ages and it can progress at different rates.
      ii. This results in judgment impairments and issues in problem solving and behavior.

2. **Alzheimer's Disease**
   a. Alzheimer's is a TYPE of dementia and is an irreversible form caused by nerve cell deterioration.
      i. There is a steady, progressive decline in functional capacity.

Image 7.2 Brain Atrophy in Alzheimers

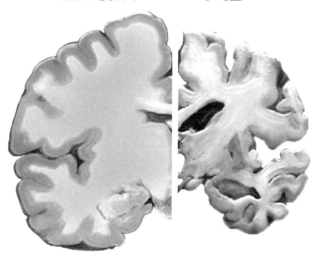

Assessment

1. *Apraxia* - difficulty performing motor tasks
2. *Aphasia* - difficulty progressing to inability to speak and understand what is being said to them
3. *Agnosia* - doesn't recognize familiar people or objects
4. *Amnesia* - memory loss

Therapeutic Management

1. **Caregiver stress**
   a. Role strain – i.e. child caring for a parent
   b. Sadness due to loved one not recognizing them
2. **Safety**
   a. Wandering can be an issue. Units should be locked/secured, clients should be supervised.
   b. Watch water temperature – may burn themselves
   c. Remove anything toxic or hazardous from easy access
   d. Watch for agitation
      i. Remove things that increase agitation
   e. Decrease stimuli/reassure the client
   f. Never argue
   g. Use a calm, reassuring voice with gentle touch (when appropriate)
   h. Watch for sundowning
      i. Increased confusion at night
3. **Communicate**
   a. Maintain eye contact
   b. Stand in front of them, be calm, firm, and direct with communication and tasks
   c. Simple one-step tasks/direction
   d. Use short, simple words
   e. Always identify them and yourself
   f. Reorient as needed, which may be frequent
4. **Promote their current abilities**
   a. Keep familiar things around them
   b. Continually reinforce what they know and can do at this point in time
   c. Promote independence, supervise to ensure ADL's are taken care of

d. Utilize familiar simple games and activities they enjoy

    i. Coloring, reading books they enjoy

    ii. Talk about their memories

    iii. Maintain routine

    iv. Pay attention to fatigue, memory strain, and agitation and provide ample time for rest

    v. Keep a calendar and clock on the wall and refer to it when discussing the date/time

Mood Disorders

Overview

Mood - emotional states are subjective and difficult to define and are long term.

General

1. *Mood disorders*
   a. Emotional *extremes* and *challenges regulating* moods (think long-term)
      i. Example: Bipolar disorder and depressive disorders

Assessment

1. Bipolar includes periods of mania and depression with normal periods in between
   a. Extremely high highs
   b. Extremely low lows
   c. Inability to self-regulate
2. Mania definition: a mood disorder marked by hyperactive, wildly optimistic state
3. Depression: 5+ depressive symptoms for 2+ weeks

Therapeutic Management

1. **Goals**
   a. Manage acute episodes
   b. Provide support and resources for long-term management
2. **Meds**
   a. Anti-anxiety medication can be used during manic episodes. Caution should be used with clients who have a history of substance abuse
   b. Antipsychotics:
      i. olanzapine (Zyprexa), aripiprazole (Abilify), risperidone (Risperdal)
   c. Mood stabilizer
      i. Lithium
         1. Clients will need regular labs to check the therapeutic level
         2. Toxicity can result if stable sodium intake and fluid intake (2-3L/day) is not maintained
   d. sodium valproate (Depakote), lamotrigine (Lamictal), carbamazepine (Tegretol) are given to clients with mood disorders
3. **Interventions for Mania**
   a. Make sure the environment is safe, watch for dangerous hyperactivity
   b. Reorient as necessary
   c. Promote appropriate sleep/wake cycles
   d. Controlled, calm, focused interactions to help control the hyperactive personality
   e. High-calorie finger foods because they are manic and hyperactive
   f. Set boundaries related to behaviors
   g. Ensure medication compliance

Depression

Overview

State of low mood and aversion to activity that can affect a person's thoughts, behaviors, feelings, and sense of wellbeing

General

1. **Can be mild, moderate, or severe**
   a. Mild: lasts 2 weeks or less
   b. Moderate: more persistent, negative thinking and suicidal thoughts may occur
   c. Severe: intense and pervasive, may include delusions and hallucinations

Assessment

1. Some combination of the following symptoms may be present, especially in major depressive disorder
   a. Depressed mood most of the day
   b. Diminished interest or pleasure in activities
   c. Significant unintentional weight loss
   d. Insomnia or hypersomnia
   e. Psychomotor agitation
   f. Fatigue or loss of energy
   g. Feelings of worthlessness, or excessive or inappropriate guilt
   h. Difficulty concentrating or making decisions
   i. Recurrent thoughts of death or suicide, with or without a plan
   j. Low self-esteem
   k. Feelings of hopelessness
   l. Poor appetite or overeating
2. The symptoms cause clinically significant distress or impairment in social, occupational, or other important areas of functioning

Therapeutic Management

1. #1 priority is assessing the risk for self-harm: "Have you had any thoughts of hurting yourself?"
   a. If they say yes then ask, "do you have a plan?"
2. Ensure a safe environment
   a. Removing anything from their room that they could potentially use to harm themselves
3. Promote appropriate intake – focus on higher-calorie foods frequently
   a. They may go long periods without eating so maximize intake when they actually do eat.
4. May need reminding/encouragement to maintain basic personal hygiene (ADL's)
5. Encourage expression of feelings and focus on their strengths
6. Validate their feelings of loss/frustration/sadness
7. Promote spending time with them to show them they are a priority to you
8. Engage the client in activity toward progress
   a. One-on-one situations, eventually progressing to group discussions
   b. Start with gross motor activities
   c. Suggest activities that are easy to complete, non-competitive, and that offer a sense of accomplishment when complete (coloring, drawing, playing cards, easy games)
9. Promote appropriate sleep-wake cycles

Suicidal Behavior

Overview

Clients with a consistent feeling of hopelessness, guilt, and worthlessness that are so overwhelming that they don't want to live anymore and attempt to end their life

General

1 At Risk Clients

   a People with a previous history of suicide, family history of suicide, mental illness history

      i. Personality disorders

      ii. Substance abuse

      iii. Psychosis

      iv. People with depression

      v. People with terminal illness

      vi. People with disabilities

      vii. Elderly and adolescents

Assessment

1. **Objective information**

   a. When they give away important, prized possessions

   b. Creating a will or changing an existing one

   c. Sleep disturbances

   d. Difficulty concentrating, loss of interest in things

   e. Asking about methods to end one's life

   f. Writing notes to loved ones

   g. Sudden massive improvements in previously very depressed clients

      i. Clients may have motivation/energy, or relief because they came up with a plan or made a decision.

      ii. Observe the client more closely for potential increased probability of carrying out the plan.

Therapeutic Management

1. *Assessment*

   a. Assess clients with a history of depression for risk for suicide and self-harm

2. *Safety is Essential*

   a. Inpatients admitted with suicide attempts are not to be left alone, any items that could be used for self-harm are removed from their room

3. *Initiate suicide precautions*

   a. Typically includes removing all objects that could be used to harm self from the room

4. *Begin Sitter or 1:1 supervision*

   a. Never leave the client alone

5. *Other Therapeutic Management*

   a. Establish a suicide contract

   b. Establish rapport and trust

   c. Provide positive reinforcement

   d. Involve the support system the client identifies

   e. Encourage therapy (individual, group)

Post-Traumatic Stress Disorder (PTSD)

Overview

A mental illness that results after someone experiences trauma.

General

1. The client might relive the trauma, frequently dream about it, or have flashbacks
2. Traumatic events that cause PTSD include anything traumatic to the client such as rape, accidents, wartime experiences, or natural disasters

Assessment

1. The client might experience sleep issues such as insomnia, nightmares, and flashbacks
2. The client might develop mental health issues such as depression or anxiety
3. The client might avoid triggers
   a. A trigger is a situational, audible, or visual experience (among others) which invokes an anxiety-driven or fear response, similar to the original occurrence or cause of the PTSD.
   b. For example, if a client was subjected to violence at a particular location, they may avoid that location or similar locations, knowing that the situation may cause anxiety-like symptoms.
4. The client might have guilt related to the event
   a. For example, if they survived and others did not, the client might have thoughts that they could have done something differently.

Therapeutic Management

1. Validate the client's feelings and promote coping mechanisms that work for them
2. Offer relaxation techniques
3. Encourage outpatient therapy and support groups
4. Therapy/service animals may help clients

Anxiety

Overview

- A sense of worry or nervousness, typically about an upcoming event with an uncertain outcome.

- Anxiety is a normal part of life, but becomes concerning when it is persistent, chronic, and/or is a response to normal life activities.

General

1. **Types of anxiety**
   a. Normal: healthy
   b. Acute: sudden, related to an event/threat (also normal)
   c. Chronic: consistent, related to normal daily activities

Assessment

1. **Levels**
   a. Mild: can be healthy, motivating, and produce growth
   b. Moderate: can still function and solve problems/issues
   c. Severe: individual needs someone to refocus them
   d. Panic: dread, impending doom, and lack of rational thoughts - this can lead to exhaustion

Therapeutic Management

1. **Therapeutic interventions**
   a. Ensure safety
   b. Provide a calming and safe environment
   c. Establish trust and acknowledge the anxiety
   d. Encourage expression of thoughts, feelings, and problem-solving
   e. Promote their coping mechanisms; do not critique/criticize
   f. Provide gross motor activities to reduce stress
      i. Definition: movement and coordination of arms, legs, and large body parts
      ii. Examples: running, walking, jumping

   g. Give anti-anxiety meds PRN

2. **Interventions for an acute anxiety attack**
   a. Decrease stimuli and maintain a calm environment
      i. Overstimulation makes it worse
   b. Encourage the client to identify and discuss feelings and their causes
      i. This helps them to see connections between the behaviors and their resulting feelings
   c. Listen/watch for indications of risk for self-harm like helplessness and hopelessness
      i. Safety is the priority

Hemophilia

Overview

1. Impairment of the body's ability to control blood clotting due to deficiency in specific clotting proteins.
2. X-linked recessive disorder (hereditary disorder)
   a. Carrier females pass to a male

General

1. **Types**
   a. *Hemophilia A (deficiency of factor VIII)*
   b. *Hemophilia B (deficiency of factor IX)*
   c. *Hemophilia C (deficiency of factor XI)*
2. **Clotting Cascade**
   a. Missing coagulation factors which prevent fibrin formation
   b. Hemophiliacs bleed for a long time because they can NOT clot

Assessment

1. **Common concerns are epistaxis (nose bleeds) and prolonged bleeding due to trauma**
2. **Frequent bruising**
3. **Areas of concern**
   a. *Bleeding in the brain*
      i. Visual changes
      ii. Headaches
      iii. Change in LOC
      iv. Slurred speech
   b. *GI Bleed*
      i. Hematemesis – throwing up blood
      ii. Melena – black stools = upper GI bleed.
4. **Normal PT and thrombin time, prolonged PTT**

Therapeutic Management

1. **Goal of Therapy**
   a. Replace missing clotting factors
   b. Prevent bleeding
   c. Prevent long term problems with joints
2. **Medications**
   a. Replace the missing factor→ Slow IV push
   b. DDAVP→ Increases the body's production of clotting factor and is ONLY used in mild Hemophilia A
3. **Many clients will have a metaport for access**
   a. Be sure to maintain sterility when accessed
   b. Only access when following policies or orders

Congenital Heart Defects

Overview

1. *Congenital heart defects*
   a. Abnormalities in the structure of the heart
   b. Caused by improper development during gestation
2. *Associated with*
   a. Chromosomal abnormalities, syndromes, congenital defects.
3. *Risk factors*
   a. Parent or sibling has a heart defect
   b. Maternal diabetes
   c. Maternal use of alcohol and illicit drugs
   d. Exposures to infections in utero (rubella)

General

1. Congenital Heart Defects can be classified by answering the following question:
   a. How does it affect hemodynamics (blood flow patterns) in the heart?
      i. *Increased pulmonary blood flow*
         1. Atrial Septal Defect
         2. Ventricular Septal Defect
         3. Patent ductus arteriosus
         4. Atrioventricular canal
      ii. *Decreased pulmonary blood flow*
         1. Tetralogy of Fallot
         2. Tricuspid atresia
      iii. *Obstruction to blood flow*
         1. Coarctation of the aorta
         2. Aortic stenosis
         3. Pulmonic stenosis
      iv. *Mixed blood flow*
         1. Transposition of great arteries
         2. Truncus arteriosus
         3. Hypoplastic Left Heart

Assessment

1. General Signs and Symptoms
   a. Murmurs
   b. Additional heart sounds
   c. Irregular rhythms
   d. Clubbing of fingers and toes
   e. Failure to thrive
2. Signs of Heart Failure
   a. *Poor myocardial function*
      i. Tachycardia
      ii. Gallop rhythm
      iii. Sweating (while feeding)
      iv. Decreased urinary output
      v. Fatigue
      vi. Pale, cool extremities
      vii. Hypotension
      viii. Cyanosis
   b. *Respiratory congestion (left-sided heart failure)*
      i. Tachypnea
      ii. Dyspnea
      iii. Grunting
      iv. Retractions
      v. Nasal flaring
      vi. Exercise intolerance (older children)
      vii. Feeding intolerance (infants)
      viii. Cyanosis
      ix. Cough
      x. Wheezing
   c. *Systemic congestion*
      i. Weight gain
      ii. Enlarged liver
      iii. Peripheral edema
         1. Periorbital
         2. Sacral (infants lying down)

Therapeutic Management

1. Surgery
2. Cardiac catheterization
3. Common Medications
   a. Digoxin

      i. Signs of toxicity

      ii. Medication orders must specify HR parameters for holding medication.

         1. This is due to HR variations with age.

  b. Ace Inhibitors, beta-blockers, diuretics

4. Nursing Care

  a. Decrease Cardiac Demands

      i. Conserve energy for feeds

      ii. Minimize stress

  b. Minimize Respiratory Distress

      i. Elevate the head of the bed

      ii. Administer Oxygen

  c. Support Adequate Nutrition

      i. Feed infants every 3 hours→ do not last longer than 30 minutes

      ii. High-calorie formulas

  d. Monitor Fluids and Electrolytes

      i. Daily weight

      ii. Strict I's & O's

      iii. Potassium

Cheatsheet 5.3 Congenital Heart Defects

CONGENITAL HEART DEFECTS

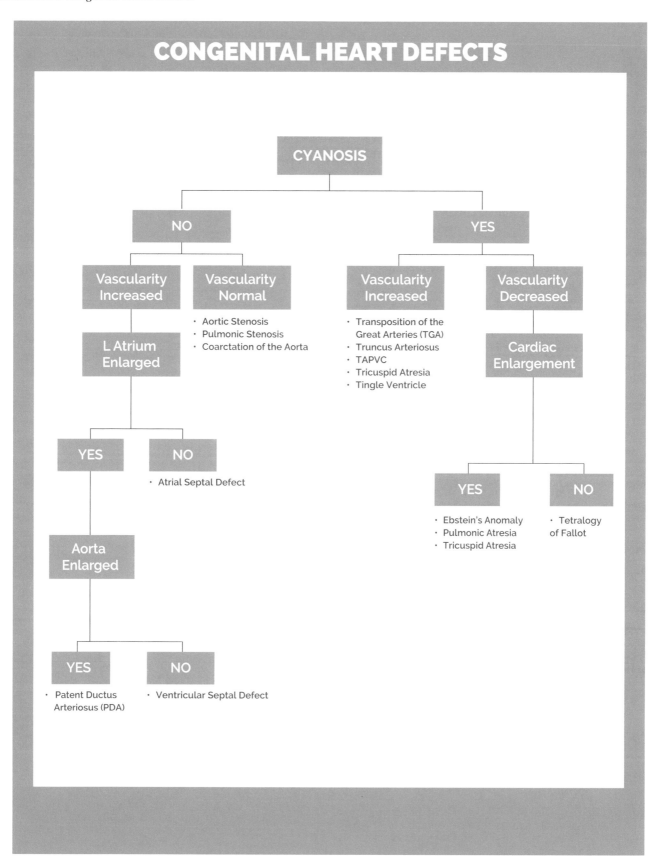

CYANOSIS

NO

YES

Vascularity Increased

Vascularity Normal
- Aortic Stenosis
- Pulmonic Stenosis
- Coarctation of the Aorta

Vascularity Increased
- Transposition of the Great Arteries (TGA)
- Truncus Arteriosus
- TAPVC
- Tricuspid Atresia
- Tingle Ventricle

Vascularity Decreased

L Atrium Enlarged

Cardiac Enlargement

YES

NO
- Atrial Septal Defect

YES
- Ebstein's Anomaly
- Pulmonic Atresia
- Tricuspid Atresia

NO
- Tetralogy of Fallot

Aorta Enlarged

YES
- Patent Ductus Arteriosus (PDA)

NO
- Ventricular Septal Defect

NURSING.com NCLEX Flash Notes | Save 50% on Lifetime
NURSING.com Membership at NURSING.com/book
105

Gestational Diabetes

Overview

1. Pregnancy can cause insulin resistance because increased weight and hormones cause higher blood sugars
2. but needs a source for glucose.
3. If the mother has high blood sugar, the glucose will cross the placenta.
   a. In response to the mother's hyperglycemia, the fetus's body produces more insulin causing excessive growth.
   b. Maternal insulin will not cross the placenta, only the glucose.

Assessment

1. **Maternal changes are as follows:**
   a. 1st trimester: insulin needs are reduced
   b. 2nd and 3rd trimester: insulin resistance occurs when hormones increase
      i. Insulin needs increase
   c. Right after placenta delivers: hormones and insulin requirements decrease
      i. Gestational diabetics should no longer require insulin or diet management post-delivery
2. **Newborn changes/issues**
   a. The baby grows faster and larger, but their function is still reflective of age and not size
   b. Macrosomic = 4000g
3. **Assessments**
   a. Screen for glucose and protein in urine at regular prenatal visits (glucosuria and ketonuria)
   b. Check blood sugar between 24-28 weeks with glucola testing
   c. High-risk patients may be screened at the beginning of pregnancy.

Therapeutic Management

1. Ideal to control with diet and exercise
2. Monitor for typical DM complications (signs of infection, HTN, edema, proteinuria)

Preeclampsia

Overview

1. Hypertensive disorder (140/90)
2. Proteinuria
3. After 20 weeks gestation

General

1. A woman may or may not be symptomatic but will have elevated blood pressures and proteinuria

    a. Proteinuria - >300 mg in a 24 hr urine specimen and a Protein:Creatinine Ratio of >0.3

2. Blood pressures

    a. 140/90 or more for two occurrences

        i. 4 hours apart

    b. Or a systolic 160 mmHg or more

    c. Or a diastolic of 90 mmHg or more

        i. 140/90 & 160/90 are both classified as preeclamptic hypertension

Assessment

1. **So what does this client look like?**

    a. A sudden increase in edema

        i. Displayed in hands and face

    b. Sudden weight gain

        i. Occurs in excess fluid retention

    c. Complaints of headache, epigastric, or RUQ pain

    d. Vision changes

        i. A serious symptom of preeclampsia

        ii. From swelling and irritation of the brain and the CNS

    e. Proteinuria→ MUST be present to be preeclampsia

2. **Fetal assessment**

    a. Intrauterine growth restriction (IUGR)

        i. Placental blood flow is not at its best

Therapeutic Management

1. Delivery of the baby is the only treatment
2. Magnesium sulfate is given prophylactically

    a. Seizure prevention

3. Some antihypertensive drugs might be given to manage BP

Infections in Pregnancy

Overview

1. Specific infections during pregnancy are more concerning due potential transmission to the fetus (via placenta or during delivery), which can have detrimental effects on the newborn

2. **TORCH**
   a. T - Toxoplasmosis
   b. O - Other
      i. ie: Group B strep (GBS), HIV, Syphilis
   c. R - Rubella
   d. C - Cytomegalovirus
   e. H - Herpes simplex

General

1. **Toxoplasmosis**
   a. Parasitic disease transmitted to mother while handling cat litter, undercooked or raw meat, or gardening; transmitted to fetus via the placenta
   b. Mother is typically asymptomatic but may have a rash or flu-like symptoms for anywhere from a few weeks to months
   c. Fetal death, spontaneous abortion, and neuro complications may result
   d. Educate the mother to never change cat litter

2. **Other**
   a. *Group-B Strep*
      i. All women screened for this during the prenatal period by a vaginal swab 35-37 weeks
      ii. All women have the bacteria but the results will depend on the amount that is colonized
      iii. Prophylactic antibiotics (penicillin or ampicillin) given during labor to women who screen positive
      iv. Main cause of bacterial infections in newborns, which causes sepsis
   b. *HIV*
      i. Delivery by c/s to limit transmission
      ii. Infants are given antiretrovirals

   c. *Syphilis*
      i. Woman given penicillin and fetus receives penicillin after delivery

3. **Rubella**
   a. Transmitted via placenta
   b. Most dangerous/serious if mother acquires this infection in 1st trimester
   c. Brain damage, hearing loss, miscarriage, stillbirth, and various congenital defects may result
   d. Assess the mother's immunity by drawing titer. If her titer is non-immune, then vaccinate immediately after delivery because it is a live vaccine.
      i. The vaccine will protect for future pregnancies

4. **Cytomegalovirus (CMV)**
   a. A very common, asymptomatic virus transmitted through bodily fluids
   b. Transmitted via placenta or during delivery and can cause intrauterine growth restriction, seizures, blindness, hepatomegaly, splenomegaly, jaundice, hearing loss, microcephaly, and/or death

5. **Herpes Simplex**
   a. Transmitted during birth, if active lesions present. A c-section should be done if active lesion to prevent transmission
   b. Acyclovir may be given around 36 weeks to prevent an outbreak during labor and delivery
   c. Serious neonatal complications (death, neurologic issues, etc.)

Newborn Physical Exam

Overview

1. These are the first physical assessments – establishing a baseline is important!
2. Assess for temperature stability and note ALL abnormalities

General

1. Keep baby warm!
   a. It's imperative that nursing interventions are made to maintain temperature stability
2. The intrauterine – extrauterine transition period
   a. 3 phases
      i. Reactivity
         1. *Most alert and is the best feeding time*
         2. *First hour*
      ii. Decreased responsiveness
         1. Sleepy
         2. Second hour
      iii. Reactivity
         1. Second reactivity
         2. Hour 2-6
         3. Alert

Assessment

1. **General observations**
   a. Newborns should have a flexed posture & coordinated movements
   b. Count extremities, fingers, toes
   c. Check for anus → *not patent then DO NOT feed*
      i. **If no anus is found, this results in an emergent surgery!**
   d. Urinary meatus on the penis if male
      i. Hypospadias is meatus on the under portion
         1. **NO CIRCUMCISION can be performed on these clients**
   e. Check for hip dysplasia (hip pops)
      i. Assessed with the Ortolani maneuver
         1. Rotate thighs outward and feel for clicks at the hips,
         2. NO clicking or crepitus is a normal finding
         3. Any clicking or crepitus is indicative of hip dysplasia
         4. Hip dysplasia is also checked by putting the infant prone and looking for symmetrical butt creases
            a. Symmetry indicates no dysplasia

2. **Vital signs**
   a. Some newborns may present with *slight/subtle tremors*
      i. Can be normal or can be due to drugs withdrawal, hypocalcemia, or hypoglycemia
   b. Listen to *apical pulse* for 1 full min
      i. 120-160 BP resting is a normal finding
   c. Listen to *respirations* for 1 full min
      i. 30-60 RR is a normal finding
   d. Axillary temp
      i. 97.8-99F is a normal finding

3. **Head**
   a. Measure head, weight, length
   b. Fontanels (soft spot) anterior (back of the head) and posterior (top of the head)

4. **Eyes**
   a. Weak eye muscle
   b. Newborns may have strabismus or disconjugate gaze

5. **Ears**
   a. No pits or skin tags

6. **Mouth**
   a. Assess for an intact palate, no teeth

7. **Chest**
   a. Assess for clavicular fractures from birth
   b. Breast tissue swelling might be observed
   c. May note secretions from the nipple

8. **Umbilical cord**
   a. *Assess for 2 arteries and 1 vein*
      i. Assess for meconium staining on the cord

b.

AVA

- Way to remember how many arteries and veins in the umbilical cord – 2 **Arteries** & 1 **Vein**

 A Artery

 V Vein

 A Artery

9. **Genitalia**
   a. Female
      i. blood-stained discharge may be present due to a sudden decrease of estrogen
      ii. might be swollen, prominent labia majora
   b. Male
      i. Hydrocele – excess fluid in the scrotum

10. **Skin**
    a. Should have creases on hands and feet
       i. More creases indicate an older gestational age

11. **Possible skin findings in a newborn:**
    a. *Erythema toxicum*
       i. Normal newborn rash→ Red spots that pop up and move to different spots
    b. *Acrocyanosis*
       i. Blue extremities
       ii. Normal for the first few days
    c. *Lanugo*
       i. Fine body hair
    d. *Harlequin Sign*
       i. Red/pink on one half of body
       ii. Other half is normal or pallor is present
       iii. Indicative of cardiac issues or sepsis
    e. *Milia*
       i. Small white sebaceous glands
       ii. Typically noted on the face
    f. *Vernix caseosa*
       i. Protective mechanism
       ii. White, cheese-looking substance

iii. Term
    1. Preterm – typically covered
    2. Term – typically only in folds
    3. Postterm – absent
g. *Stork bites*
    i. Nape of neck, nose, eyelids
    ii. Dark red – pale pink
h. *Port-wine stain*
    i. Nevus vasculosus, typically on the face
    ii. Flat, red-purple
    iii. Technically a capillary angioma below the skin
i. *Mongolian spots*
    i. On the back, bottom
    ii. Black – blue
    iii. Flat, wavy borders and irregular shape
    iv. More common in darker races (African, Asian, Native American)

Cheatsheet 4.8 Newborn Assessment

NEWBORN ASSESSMENT

APGAR Score

Appearance		1 Minute	5 Minutes
Pink torso and extremities	2		
Pink torso, blue extremities	1		
Blue all over	0		
Pulse		1 Minute	5 Minutes
> 100	2		
< 100	1		
Absent	0		
Grimace		1 Minute	5 Minutes
Vigorous cry	2		
Limited cry	1		
No response to stimulus	0		
Activity		1 Minute	5 Minutes
Actively moving	2		
Limited movement	1		
Flaccid	0		
Respiratory Effort		1 Minute	5 Minutes
Strong loud cry	2		
Hypoventilation, irregular	1		
Absent	0		
Total:			

8-10 normal, 4-6 moderate depression, 0-3 aggressive resuscitation

Normal Measurements

Weight: 6-10 lbs.
Length: 18-22 in.
Head circumference: 33-35 cm.
Chest circumference: 30-33 cm.

Meds and Labs

Vitamin K: prevent hemorrhage
Optic Antibiotic: prevent newborn blindness
PKU Level: within 24 hrs after feeding begins
Coombs' Test: if mother Rh-neg.
Immunizations: Hep-B can be given

Newborn Assessment

Appearance: pink, loud cry, well-flexed, full ROM

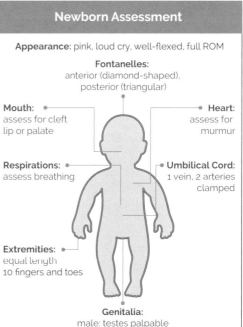

Fontanelles: anterior (diamond-shaped), posterior (triangular)

Mouth: assess for cleft lip or palate

Heart: assess for murmur

Respirations: assess breathing

Umbilical Cord: 1 vein, 2 arteries clamped

Extremities: equal length 10 fingers and toes

Genitalia:
male: testes palpable
female: discharge of blood or mucus normal

Fontanelles

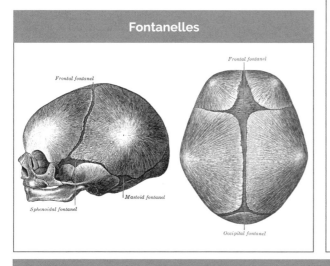

Frontal fontanel
Frontal fontanel
Mastoid fontanel
Sphenoidal fontanel
Occipital fontanel

Possible Complications During Delivery

Meconium Aspiration
Cord Presentation
Breech Presentation

Limb Presentation
Postpartum Hemorrhage

NURSING.com NCLEX Flash Notes | Save 50% on Lifetime
NURSING.com Membership at NURSING.com/book
111

Chorioamnionitis

Overview

1. Intrauterine infection of the chorion, amnion or fetal membranes.
2. Classified with high maternal fever, fetal tachycardia, maternal tachycardia, or foul smell.

General

1. **Causes**
   a. Intrauterine or invasive procedure
      i. Cervical exams (foreign body inserted causing infection)
      ii. Amniocentesis (because a foreign needle is inserted in the sac)
      iii. Prolonged rupture of membranes (more opportunity for bacteria to enter)
2. **Can result in endometritis and sepsis**

Assessment

1. **Diagnostics**
   a. Fever over 100.4° F + two of the following:
      i. Leukocytosis
      ii. Maternal tachycardia
      iii. Malodorous amniotic fluid
      iv. Fetal tachycardia
2. **Monitor vitals of mother and fetus for S/S of sepsis or fetal distress**
   a. Maternal tachycardia
   b. Maternal temperature
   c. Fetal tachycardia or decelerations
3. **Draw blood cultures promptly if suspected – *BEFORE* antibiotics are initiated**
4. **Mother treated primarily with ampicillin and gentamicin.**
5. **After delivery, the infant might be treated also depending on symptoms**

Image 4.4 Chorioamnionitis

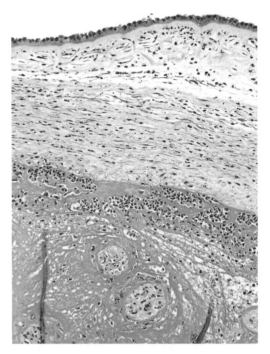

By Nephron - Own work, CC BY-SA 3.0, https://commons.wikimedia.org/w/index.php?curid=16158284

Made in the USA
Columbia, SC
20 May 2024

35910964R00063